GLOBAL TELECOM TALKS
A Trillion Dollar Deal

BEN PETRAZZINI

GLOBAL TELECOM TALKS
A Trillion Dollar Deal

INSTITUTE FOR INTERNATIONAL ECONOMICS
Washington, DC
June 1996

Ben A. Petrazzini is Assistant Professor at the Department of Information and Systems Management of The Hong Kong University of Science and Technology. Mr. Petrazzini holds a Ph.D. in Communication from the University of California, San Diego, a law degree from National University of Córdoba, a MA in Sociology, and a MA in Social Sciences. He served as an adviser to the National Congress of Argentina, and taught at the National University of Buenos Aires. He has done extensive research on the reform of the telecommunications sector of developing countries. An early version of his book, "The Political Economy of Telecommunications Reform in Developing Countries," won the 1993 Pacific Telecommunications Council Research Prize. His most recent work includes "Hong Kong's Information Infrastructure," "Telecommunications Policy in India: The Political Underpinnings of Reform," "Foreign Direct Investment in Latin America's Privatization," "The Privatization of Telecommunications Services: The Case of Argentina," "Labor: A Post-Privatization Assesment," and several other papers on Asia's telecommunications markets. He has also consulted for the Mexican government and private enterprises on telecommunications and regional economic integration.

INSTITUTE FOR INTERNATIONAL ECONOMICS
11 Dupont Circle, NW
Washington, DC 20036-1207
(202) 328-9000 FAX: (202) 328-5432
http://www.iie.com

C. Fred Bergsten, *Director*
Christine F. Lowry, *Director of Publications*

Printing and Typesetting by
Automated Graphic Systems

Printed in the United States of America
98 97 96 5 4 3 2 1

Library of Congress Cataloging-in-Publication Data

Petrazzini, Ben A.
   Global Telecom Talks: A Trillion Dollar
   Deal
Ben Petrazzini
   p. cm.—(Policy analyses in
international economics ; 44)
   Includes bibliographical references
   1. Telecommunication—United
States—Rates. 2. Telephone—Rates—
Government policy—United States.
3. Telephone—Deregulation—United
States.
   I. Petrazzini, Ben. II. Series.

HE7787.E74 1996
384'.041—dc20   96-7611
                                                    CIP

ISBN 0-88132-230-X

Contents

Preface

After decades of peace and quiet as a protected and monopolized industry in nearly every country, the telecommunications sector has become a high-powered driver of national competitiveness and global integration. The scope of telecommunications services now ranges from meeting the most basic human needs to linking sophisticated financial markets and manufacturing enterprises worldwide. Over the past two decades, the cost of data communications has dropped by three orders of magnitude, providing fuel for competition across a wide range of economic activities. Many of the recent technological leaps and competitive changes, however, have happened *despite* public policy rather than because of it.

In January 1996, the Institute for International Economics hosted a telecommunications conference in Washington. The purpose in bringing together preeminent experts was to identify the trends, clarify the issues, and make recommendations for upcoming international negotiations both in the World Trade Organization (WTO) and in regional groups such as the Asia Pacific Economic Cooperation forum (APEC) and the newly formed Free Trade Area of the Americas (FTAA). The Institute commissioned this monograph by Ben Petrazzini, drawing on the conference papers, his own experience, and latest reports from the WTO negotiations, in order to provide a larger audience a ringside view of the technological, political, and economic changes sweeping the industry.

Petrazzini's monograph helps dispel pervasive myths that continue to impede negotiations—notably, the notion that telecom liberalization will cause a net employment loss in the sector and the belief that liberalization and universal service are antagonistic rather than allied concepts. Indeed, the monograph makes clear that expanded service has *followed* liberalization and that postliberalization service is substantially better in quality and lower in price. Higher teledensity rates and a rapidly expanding range of value-added products stimulate growth in other sectors of the economy, especially those that compete internationally.

A key objective of this monograph is to encourage progress in the WTO negotiations, which deadlocked 30 April 1996, as they shoot for a new deadline of 15 February 1997. These talks are the single most important global trade negotiations now under way, and are closely watched as a bellwether for the WTO's ability to conclude sectoral negotiations more broadly. The Institute hopes that this monograph will assist the countries in reaching a successful outcome and thereby contribute to the WTO as it evolves in the post-Uruguay Round world.

The Institute for International Economics is a private nonprofit institution for the study and discussion of international economic policy. Its purpose is to analyze important issues in that area and to develop and communicate practical new approaches for dealing with them. The Institute is completely nonpartisan.

The Institute is funded largely by philanthropic foundations. Major institutional grants are now being received from the German Marshall Fund of the United States, which created the Institute with a generous commitment of funds in 1981, and from the Ford Foundation, the Andrew Mellon Foundation, and the C. V. Starr Foundation. A number of other foundations and private corporations also contribute to the highly diversified financial resources of the Institute. About 16 percent of the Institute's resources in our latest fiscal year were provided by contributors outside the United States, including about 7 percent from Japan.

The Board of Directors bears overall responsibility for the Institute and gives general guidance and approval to its research program—including identification of topics that are likely to become important to international economic policymakers over the medium run (generally, one to three years), and which thus should be addressed by the Institute. The Director, working closely with the staff and outside Advisory Committee, is responsible for the development of particular projects and makes the final decision to publish an individual study.

The Institute hopes that its studies and other activities will contribute to building a stronger foundation for international economic policy around the world. We invite readers of these publications to let us know how they think we can best accomplish this objective.

C. FRED BERGSTEN
Director
May 1996

Acknowledgments

I would like to thank the people who contributed to the production of this volume on an expedited schedule. C. Fred Bergsten and the Institute for International Economics invited me to their January 1996 conference on telecommunications and suggested that this summary book be written. The scholarship and views exchanged at the conference by numerous participants provided important evidence used in this study. Subsequently, the manuscript benefited from detailed comments from Carlos Primo Braga of the World Bank, Peter Cowhey of the Federal Communications Commission, and Judith O'Neill of Reid & Priest. Gary Hufbauer, Daniel Rosen, and Gautam Jaggi of the Institute for International Economics provided substantial comment. Other Institute staff, including Fred Bergsten, Geoffrey Carliner, Jeffrey J. Schott, and Ellen Frost read earlier versions of the study, and I thank them for their comments and suggestions.

1

A Snapshot of the Telecommunications Revolution

Global negotiations on liberalization of trade in telecommunications recently deadlocked, prompting a last-minute 10-month extension of the 30 April 1996 deadline. Originally part of the Uruguay Round's General Agreement on Trade in Services (GATS), the telecom sector proved too contentious for the round itself. Consequently, the Negotiating Group on Basic Telecommunications (NGBT) was launched to continue discussions. The group included 53 participants plus 24 observer nations—big and small, economically advanced and less developed. Its new target date for completing negotiations is 15 February 1997.

The NGBT talks are by far the most important negotiation the World Trade Organization (WTO) has conducted since its inception. Despite the concerted push given to the NGBT by WTO Director General Renato Ruggiero and by leaders of the "Quad" governments,[1] the achievements fell far short of the ambitious goal of reaching agreement on a timetable for open and competitive telecommunications worldwide.

This study explains why so much attention has gone into basic telecommunications—the local and long-distance voice and data transmission services that have long been regarded as a dull utility sector. The explanation has multiple parts, but the sum of them is clear: the WTO negotiations were driven by powerful forces that are changing the way basic telecom services are delivered—forces that are increasing the importance of basic

---

1. The Quad comprises the United States, Japan, Germany (as EU representative), and Canada. It is an informal caucus of leading economies convened to share views on trade policy and set priorities.

telecom in an emerging global information-based economy and ultimately reconfiguring the way people work and live.

Behind the Dial Tone

Technological change is not always seamless. Often it occurs in spurts. The light bulb, teamed with electricity, put candle makers out of business, bringing enormous benefit to consumers, and simultaneously increasing productivity and social development. Modern telecommunications technology is no less dramatic.

Isolated villages that have waited decades for telephone service are suddenly finding wireless phone service at their doorsteps, ahead of long-promised copper cables. Satellite-based systems will soon deliver calls from any point on the earth to any other. New technologies are leap-frogging existing networks and providing entire regions with affordable, quality telecom service—many for the first time.

The traditional system of a monopoly public telephone operator, or PTO, that is closely associated with its regulatory agency, is slow to innovate, and is careless about costs. Therefore, as this study shows, it needs to be replaced. Consider the following:

- **The uses of telecom services are changing dramatically, away from voice service and toward data**. Costs for voice communications have declined by a factor of 10 in real terms over the past two decades. Meanwhile, the cost of data communications has fallen by a factor of 1,000—fueling a new breed of services to access the Internet and to take advantage of multimedia technology, for instance.

- **There is room for more competition on rates.** As recently as 1994, the charge per minute for a call from London to New York was about 60 cents, when the underlying costs were close to 10 cents—a 500 percent markup.

- **Competition cuts the cost of services**. Competition brings cost savings. Call-back services are leveling the playing field and forcing down prices, even where nations try to protect national monopolies.

- **Telecom service expands rapidly with liberalization.** The number of phones per hundred households (known as teledensity) in developing countries has grown twice as fast in countries with privatized telecommunications as in countries that did not privatize.

- **Overall telecom employment tends to increase—not diminish—in liberalized telecom markets.** A study of 26 Latin American and Asian countries found that average telecom sector employment has grown rather than declined over the last five years. The same is true in OECD

Table 1.1   Projected benefits to users from competitive telecom services in 2010 and cumulative gains, 1997-2010[a]
(billions of dollars)

	Cost savings 2010	Quality benefits 2010	Total gains 2010	Cumulative gains[b] 1997-2010
Income level				
Low	10	15	25	177
Middle	25	25	49	346
High	50	25	75	523
Totals	85	65	149	1,046
Region/country				
European Union[c]	27	14	41	288
Latin America	9	9	17	120
East Asia and Pacific	12	18	30	211
Japan	19	10	29	201
South Asia	3	5	8	56
Rest of world	14	10	24	169

a. Excludes nations presumed to be competitive: the United States, Canada, the United Kingdom, Denmark, Finland, New Zealand, and Sweden.
b. Calculated by straight-line cumulation of benefits over the 14 years, inclusive, starting with zero in 1997 and ending with $149 bilion in 2010.
c. Refers only to the less competitive European nations: Austria, Belgium, France, Germany, Ireland, Italy, Netherlands, and Spain.

Source: Prepared by Gary Hufbauer, Institute for International Economics. Based on data in Pepper (1995), and the World Bank's *World Development Report 1995.* For methodological details, see appendix A.

countries—competition boosted employment levels in the sector overall, even while the dominant PTOs shed workers.

All this adds to a simple proposition. The enduring notion that monopoly PTOs can best provide universal, high-quality telecom service at reasonable rates to businesses and households while providing job stability and new opportunities for telecom workers is no longer valid. Therefore, protecting monopoly PTOs from competition is an undesirable, perhaps untenable, strategy.

Table 1.1 conservatively estimates the cost savings and quality benefits for 1997–2010 that would accrue if procompetitive policies and regulations were agreed and implemented expeditiously. While the projections are rough, they suggest that users will enjoy very large gains if liberalization can soon be achieved on a global scale.

Many of the gains would be enjoyed by low- and middle-income countries in, for example, Latin America, East Asia, and South Asia. Over 14 years, cumulative cost savings and quality benefits of $50 billion to $200 billion might be achieved in these three regions. Overall global gains could well exceed $1 trillion. Even allowing for estimation errors, this is a huge figure, and goes far to explain why the NGBT talks are so critical. If $1 trillion-plus can be created with new technology and squeezed out of unproductive telecom providers and delivered to consumers and businesses, then the effort spent negotiating a WTO telecom agreement to accelerate that process will be well justified.

New Challenges for Policymakers

It is easy to understand why the United States, the United Kingdom, and other telecom pioneers want open market competition. Their telecom firms are well positioned to operate globally, offering end-to-end service to firms and households around the world. But what is in it for countries that are behind the technology curve and still shelter monopoly PTOs?

The answer is to be found in what competition does for the entire economy. High-tech firms are bringing prosperity to enclaves in lower-income nations. Creating computer software is big business in India. Computer assembly is an economic dynamo in the special economic zones of China. Competitive, job-creating industries are willing to consider the cost savings and market benefits of locating anywhere, provided the telecom infrastructure is there to connect them to the world. A modern, competitive telecom infrastructure is just as essential to a developing country's ability to take advantage of global markets and booming service industries as good ocean ports, airports, and serviceable roads were to agriculture and manufacturing.

Much of today's telecom technology is extremely hard to shut out. China has one of the world's most closed telecom regimes, yet it could not stem the flow of news via fax machines during the Tiananmen Square crisis of 1989. Of greater significance in market terms are call-back services. Private citizens in Argentina face very high rates for outgoing international calls. In the past, their response was to make short, infrequent calls. Today they dial numbers in the United States, let the phone ring once, and hang up. Momentarily, their phones ring back with a dial tone that lets them call anywhere in the world at low, US rates. Short of blocking all calls from the United States, Argentine operators can do little to stop such services. The Argentine government has therefore legalized the service, hoping to manage the competition in the local market. In such niches, new telecom technology will spread around the world regardless of the outcome of telecom negotiations.

But while some segments of telecommunications are vulnerable to new, often remotely cited services such as call-back and satellite, the future of telecommunications depends on technologies that require a procompetitive regulatory environment. Products such as wireless telephony, with its ability to bring isolated communities into the global network, need

regulatory support to breach anticompetitive hurdles created by dominant PTOs. Ironically, telecom regulators must become the defenders of interconnection rights and other keys to competition—otherwise, the dominant PTO will lumber along in monopolistic bliss for years to come. Procompetitive regulation is essential to foster an open and "contestable" telecommunications sector. Here is where global negotiations can play a critical role.

Many PTOs (and many captive regulators) will defend the status quo unless pushed in a new direction by WTO agreements. To be sure, whether or not the NGBT succeeds, high quality, low-cost international services will be offered by global telecom firms to large multinationals operating anywhere in the world. But services of a similar quality and cost will not be available to small and medium-sized firms or households unless a WTO agreement lays the foundation for competitive telecom environments in all the member countries.

Dispelling Objections

Several developed and developing nations have begun liberalizing their domestic telecom markets, and they have started to enjoy the benefits of competition accordingly. Why is it then that other countries have been reluctant to increase competition in their markets? Four unfounded assumptions still haunt would-be reformers:

- that telecom liberalization fails to deliver universal service at reasonable cost;
- that telecom liberalization destroys jobs and threatens the domestic telecom industry;
- that telecom liberalization enriches only big foreign telecom firms;
- that telecom liberalization is best done step by step, starting with privatization and moving cautiously to competition only years later.

The experience of many countries, both advanced and less advanced, shows that these fears are not justified and thus should not block the speedy liberalization of telecom markets in each country.

Privatization and Competition

Two prongs of liberalization are explored in this study:

- **privatization** of national telecommunications providers;
- the introduction of **competition**, by removing entry barriers.

While both strategies can help liberalize the telecom sector, the competition strategy lowers rates and improves quality more dependably. This is because privatized monopolies are likely to focus not only on efficient operations—such as speeding up the number of lines installed and shedding unnecessary workers—but also on protecting their profit margins. Indeed, they may raise prices and oppose new products—especially cellular service—that would compete with their wire-line technology. Once a state-owned PTO is privatized, procompetitive regulation is urgently required to avoid the halfway outcome: a more efficient firm, but one that still charges high rates and is slow to introduce new technology.

The WTO Role

Global telecom negotiations seek to reconcile technological developments with the need for procompetitive regulatory regimes in a changing world. If this is achieved, telecom efficiency and services will continue to improve, and corresponding benefits will be realized by many countries that are still far away from the commercial mainstream.

Given this challenge, the NGBT has debated six main objectives in support of competition (discussed in more detail in chapter 6):

- **Regulatory reform**. The regulatory agency must have autonomy, transparency, and resources to carry out its mission of fostering competitive behavior. How can the WTO ensure that regulatory bodies have these features?

- **Interconnection**. New operators must be allowed to connect with the public switched network under equitable conditions and at reasonable rates in order to create competitive markets. To what extent can the WTO agreement ensure interconnection rights and practices?

- **Structural and accounting separation**. Competition requires that companies active in different market segments—some more open to competition, some less so—create separate subsidiaries with independent management and accounts. To what extent can "cross-subsidization" that stifles competition in some segments of the telecom market be prevented by the WTO agreement?

- **Number portability**. Firms and households need to retain their familiar and long-used phone numbers if they are to shop among providers in competitive markets. What technical and policy foundations are required to ensure this?

- **Pricing policy**. So long as dominant firms control segments of the market, regulators must find the right rate formula—usually a choice between rate-of-return and price-cap approaches. Can the WTO negotiators frame rate-setting approaches that will guide individual regulatory decisions in a procompetitive direction?

■ **Accounting rate reform.** Under the outdated accounting rate system, an originating carrier pays the destination carrier a fee for completing a call. This fee bears no relationship to the rate charged by the originating carrier to its customer or the cost of completing the call. This system, which was created in a world of monopoly PTOs, endures because it operates like a cash register for those national carriers that are still monopoly providers. Once basic telecom services are opened to competition, market forces will drive call termination fees closer to marginal costs. In the meantime, can the WTO set guidelines for rates that reflect the costs of monopoly PTOs more accurately than the accounting rates prevailing today?

Deadlocked Talks

In the run-up to the 30 April 1996 deadline, telecom negotiators scrambled to achieve a successful outcome against a backdrop of increasing publicity. But at the finish, there was insufficient progress among the advanced nations—at least in the opinion of the United States—to justify a global deal. The foundation of a deal was to have been mutual, unrestricted market access and open investment among a "critical mass" of countries. Not everyone had to accept the liberalization agenda, but all OECD nations and a good number of developing countries were expected to join the deal.

Important European participants (France, Spain, and Belgium) jettisoned their investment restrictions too late to have an encouraging effect on others. Key developing Asian economies (Indonesia and Malaysia) did not make offers, while wealthy entrepôts (Hong Kong and Singapore) limited their offers in terms of market access and investment opportunities. Other wealthy nations maintained high levels of foreign investment restrictions (Canada) and firm-specific investment limits (Japan). In all, only 11 countries, including the US, offered full commitments.

The United States then withdrew its offer of open satellite market access. The tactic was partly inspired by Motorola, a big sponsor of the Iridium satellite communications project. But the broader US reasoning was that PTOs in countries that maintained their barriers might buy a piece of other global satellite systems and gain the technical ability to offer end-to-end services without simultaneously opening their own markets.

Once the US withdrew satellites, the momentum for a deal collapsed. Appendix B presents a country-by-country summary of the final offers as they stood at the April deadline. While the offers reflect considerable progress, they also suggest a job half done. Unlike the previous WTO sector talks on financial services, in which the United Kingdom cobbled together a smaller deal once the United States pulled out, the share of global telecom revenues represented by the United States (35 percent) made this approach unworkable in the telecom realm.

Two contrasting views to the US assertion that the weak EU and Asian offers were the problem have been put forth to explain the talks' failure. The chief opposing view came from the European Union. The contention of the head EU negotiator, Sir Leon Brittan, was that the United States walked away from a deal in order to serve narrow, domestic political interests. According to this perspective, US satellite service firms—notably Motorola—and other telecom companies calculated that they would do better without a deal. Against a backdrop of antiglobalization sentiments in the American public, the US trade representative was unwilling to oppose narrow US telecom interests in a presidential election year.

A hybrid view has been suggested as well. The Europeans and some others were surprised by the US decision to walk. In the past, the United States generally had been willing to make more concessions than it got, with the objective of advancing open global markets. The new thesis is that a sea change has occurred: the United States now demands full reciprocity for every trade "concession." This can be explained by better living standards in many once-poor countries, by reduced job security in the United State, and by the rise of highly competitive firms based not only in Europe, Canada, and Japan but also in Brazil, Korea, Singapore, and elsewhere.

Another Chance

Unwilling to let slip away the significant progress that had been made, Ruggiero nudged key players to extend the talks to 15 February 1997. Importantly, the implementation date for the agreement would remain as planned before: 1 January 1998. Why engage in 10 more months of talks? The argument is that several nations were hampered by pending domestic legislation affecting their negotiating positions (Australia, Brazil, South Africa, Switzerland, and Thailand), while the United States found it increasingly difficult to maintain its concessions in an election year. India, an important emerging market, was also hampered by a general election campaign. Negotiators hope that the extension will get past some of the political thunder and still provide enough time for participants to achieve ratification before the 1 January 1998 date.

The question now is whether there is adequate leverage to accomplish by February 1997 goals that could not be reached in April 1996. Perhaps not, at least not on an unconditional most-favored nation basis, particularly if the inherent structure of trade negotiations—the need for a "big package" with trade-offs across sectors—precludes success in sectoral agreements. These limitations are briefly revisited in the concluding chapter. More optimistically, with greater public understanding of the issues, talks might succeed next year simply because the merits of telecom liberalization are so persuasive for all parties.

The nature of the issues to be worked out and the stakes in the grand bargain are the subject matter of this study. The "reference paper" on procompetitive regulatory principles, issued by the chairman on 24 April 1996, incorporates many of these issues in some form or another (see appendix C). In all, 27 nations embraced these principles fully, with others ranging from partial commitment to none. With this solid block of agreement, success seems achievable. Getting more nations to agree to the principles will be a key task in the coming months.

2

Origins and Objectives of the Negotiating Group on Basic Telecommunications

The Growing Importance of Services

For most of its history, the General Agreement on Tariffs and Trade (GATT) concerned itself with liberalizing merchandise trade. The pioneering foray into services trade during the Uruguay Round (1986–94) testifies to its growing importance.[1] Services account for an estimated 70 percent of GDP in industrialized countries and about 50 percent of GDP in emerging economies. World trade in services is expanding at about 12 percent per year and now accounts for about a quarter of total trade in goods and services.

Services pose new challenges to the international trading system. Putting investment and personnel from the home country into the foreign market is usually a prerequisite for delivering services. Uneven regulatory practices can bar new entrants. Investment issues, risk factors, visa questions, and domestic regulation are relatively new questions for the international trading system.

Liberalizing trade in services was contentious from the outset. When the United States put services on the negotiating table, many developing countries were skeptical, aware that OECD countries—particularly the United States—are highly competitive providers. Initial talks were held under the auspices of a new Group of Negotiations in Services (GNS) outside, but parallel to, the regular GATT negotiations. Several rounds

---

1. Services were first formally put on the negotiating table by the United States at the 1982 GATT ministerial meeting.

of discussions were required to identify key sectors and issues. GATT member countries eventually decided to create a General Agreement on Trade in Services (GATS).[2] Member countries identified six sectors for negotiation under the GATS: telecommunications, construction, transportation, tourism, finance, and professional services.

At the completion of the Uruguay Round, the GATS became one component of the newly created umbrella, the World Trade Organization (WTO). The GATS contained a set of general obligations applying to all services. In addition, sectoral annexes were negotiated to address market access and national-treatment commitments applying to specific sectors on a country-by-country basis. Negotiations in several services sectors were not concluded, and GATS members agreed to continue work on these areas. Prominent among them is basic telecommunications—hence the ongoing efforts of the Negotiating Group on Basic Telecommunications (NGBT).

Negotiations on Liberalizing Trade in Telecommunications

Telecommunications trade received special attention from trade negotiators throughout the Uruguay Round. This reflects both the fast growth of the sector itself (expansion rates of 20 to 40 percent annually, depending on the segment and the market), and the fact that good telecommunications are critical for efficient commerce in many other goods and services.

The 1994 Marrakesh agreement placed telecom services squarely within the framework of the new WTO. Some 57 WTO members committed to liberalize, to varying degrees, their domestic, "high end" or value-added telecom markets. While these commitments will help prevent countries from backsliding during the liberalization process, many of the commitments do not increase market access or diminish discrimination against foreign firms.

While member countries committed to liberalize value-added services, they could not reach agreement on basic telecom services—that is, local and long-distance voice and data transmission. These negotiations were therefore extended until 30 April 1996 and were assigned to the new NGBT.[3] The NGBT held several meetings after its creation and picked up

2. For a detailed history of the emergence of GATS and the role of ideas in the process, see Drake and Nicolaïdis (1992). For a summary and evaluation of the Uruguay Round, see Schott (1994).

3. According to well-documented folklore, basic telecommunications became a subject of negotiations because EU Commissioner Sir Leon Brittan "challenged" US Trade Representative Carla Hills to take up the issue. She agreed, even though AT&T, the regional Bell operating companies (RBOCs), and other players in the US industry were not then ready for serious negotiations on basic telecom. Only after bitter fighting between AT&T and large users (with the RBOCs largely on the sidelines) could the negotiations go forward.

steam as the April 1996 deadline drew near. By late January 1996, 42 WTO members were full NGBT participants, and 33 of them had made offers; another 28 countries were participating in the NGBT as observers. Participants in the negotiations accounted for more than 75 percent of existing world telecommunications services but less than 14 percent of the world's population, with population being one indicator of the potential market 30 years from now.

By early February 1996, the negotiators had made progress in defining the issues. They focused on competition questions and the surrounding issues of fair interconnection, independent regulation, and the like. However, major developing countries had still not made significant offers, and even some OECD nations were reluctant to permit wide-open competition or permit significant foreign investment in their telecom sectors.

Early in 1996, US Trade Representative Mickey Kantor insisted that the United States would not sign an NGBT agreement and open its telecom market to unlimited foreign competition and investment on a most-favored nation (MFN) basis unless a "critical mass" of other countries did likewise. Kantor deliberately did not define the term "critical mass," but he made clear that the concept included the European Union, Japan, Canada, and nearly all OECD countries, as well as nations with highly developed telecom sectors such as Singapore, Korea, and Chile, and large developing countries such as Mexico, Brazil, Argentina, India, Indonesia, and Thailand. At the end of April 1996, it became apparent that "critical mass" would not be reached—despite enormous personal efforts by WTO Director General Renato Ruggiero. For one, the EU representative refused to improve its offer pending improved offers by others. Many developing countries simply stayed on the sidelines. In the end, US telecom companies coalesced around the view that "no deal would be better than a mediocre deal," and the talks were temporarily suspended.

The liberalization offers that were put on the table in the NGBT varied considerably. In Asia, Japan offered extensive liberalization of its market, while Korea kept restrictions on foreign investment. China, the biggest market of all, was not yet at the negotiating table, both because it is not a member of the WTO and because it wants to maintain a high degree of control over basic telecom services. Singapore, a highly advanced telecom nation, did not made a significant offer; nor did India, a potentially huge market. In the Western Hemisphere, Canada and the United States offered comprehensive opening of their markets, though with some investment restrictions in the case of Canada. Latin American offers were mixed, ranging from no offer to offers shy of what national law would permit (Mexico) to pledges of full liberalization by 2000 (Venezuela). Most European countries favored market liberalization, but their offers required formal approval from a European Council beset by other members (such as Spain) that were not ready to go along. Africa and the Middle East remained largely outside the bargaining process.

Principles Underlying the Negotiations

The telecom negotiations underscore the importance of three cornerstone trade concepts: the MFN principle, the national-treatment principle, and market access. In the process, the telecom negotiations raised numerous questions that must be answered before open competitive markets can be created—for example, how to establish fair rates of interconnection to the existing public switch network, how to ensure that the dominant carrier does not otherwise exclude new entrants, and how to facilitate a local "commercial presence" for foreign firms that want to offer telecom services (Cameron and Cowhey 1996).

The MFN principle requires that service suppliers from any member of the WTO be given no less favorable access than is allowed to other WTO members. Several countries currently give preferred access to certain foreign firms that operate in their domestic markets but deny equal treatment to other foreign companies. One tool of preference is permission to connect at low cost with the public switch network. Another is rationing radio frequencies for wireless telecom. While acceptable for legitimate spectrum management reasons, rationing mechanisms can easily be applied for discriminatory purposes. All discriminatory tools would eventually have to be abandoned to ensure that the MFN concept is fully implemented by the NGBT.[4]

Under the national-treatment principle, member countries must subject foreign telecom providers to conditions no more onerous than the conditions imposed on domestic providers.[5] In the concluding phase of the GATS negotiation that ended in 1994, countries could choose not to extend the national-treatment principle to all aspects of telecom operations. Most countries reserved this option on basic telecom, which inspired the follow-on round of NGBT talks. A central objective of these talks was to ensure that foreign telecom firms could operate on the same terms as the local dominant supplier.

Market access is a closely related concept: a country's commitment to open its market to service suppliers from other member countries. There is a slight difference from the national-treatment principle, however: market-access negotiations encompass the various modes of service delivery,

---

4. The qualification "eventually" must be stressed. Under the annex to draft Article II, countries can list exceptions to MFN treatment. Presumably these will be lifted in successive negotiations.

5. Strictly speaking, national treatment is not the same as the MFN obligation. A country's own PTO might not offer a certain telecom service, and the country could discriminate in terms of market access between competing foreign telecom suppliers—violating the MFN principle but not the national-treatment principle. Moreover, to entice a certain telecom firm into a segment of the market (e.g., the provision of basic service in a rural area), it might allow one foreign supplier to charge more than the rates charged by the PTO.

some of which do not exist in all countries. Market access requires commercial presence for foreign suppliers (e.g., a Motorola cellular system in remote parts of Indonesia), cross-border supply (e.g., allowing France Telecom to connect with Telmex and provide "country direct" service for French multinationals), and the extended presence of natural persons (e.g., permitting NTT engineers to work in a UK Internet joint venture partly owned by NTT).

Liberalization of domestic telecom markets is meaningful only when accompanied by regulation that effectively prevents anticompetitive practices by the dominant carrier and applies regulations in an evenhanded way to all suppliers. The regulatory process should be transparent, and the agency should be independent of political influence and the dominant carrier. The agency should possess adequate funding and staff. Meeting these requirements is a major challenge for many developing countries and some OECD countries, where regulatory agencies are often small, underfunded, and do not carry sufficient political weight.

A comprehensive agreement on basic telecommunications liberalization would benefit consumers and new entrants, and enhance economic growth. Why is this so difficult to achieve? The reason is that after decades of cartel- and monopoly-supplied telecom services (both domestic and international), it will take carefully crafted agreements to enable public telephone operators (PTOs) to make the transition to a competitive market. Some governments, as well as many PTOs, are fearful of losing revenues generated by monopoly systems. Many of the PTOs will therefore oppose this transition. National trade policy is sometimes "captured" by these special interests. The main challenge for NGBT negotiators is to present the evidence that liberalized telecommunications markets will generate benefits far in excess of transition costs—not only on a global basis, but also for each country.

3

Where Is the Industry Going?

Synergies between telecommunications and computers have led to dramatic innovations in an industry long regarded as static. The combination of technological innovation and policy change has altered the market structure of many advanced economies and is beginning to make dramatic changes in the less developed world as well. Because they start from a much lower base of installed technology, emerging countries can expect to enjoy a significant share of gains from both the new technology and new policy. An industry traditionally dominated by state-owned monopolies is now populated by joint ventures, strategic alliances, consortia, cooperation contracts, and a variety of other risk- and revenue-sharing business arrangements.

This chapter examines industry trends, concentrating on new technologies, new services, and new forms of service provision.

Emerging Technologies and Services

In recent years, the telecom sector has successfully lowered costs, introduced new technology, and expanded the reach of its networks and the types of services offered. Not all market segments have exhibited the same degree of change. For instance, data communication prices have declined dramatically, while voice prices have remained relatively stable.[1]

---

1. Clark and McKenney (1995, 21) estimate that "costs for voice communications have declined by less than one order of magnitude [i.e., by a factor of 10], but the cost of data communications has declined by nearly three orders of magnitude over the past two decades

Figure 3.1 Compound average growth rate of communication technologies by sector, 1984-95

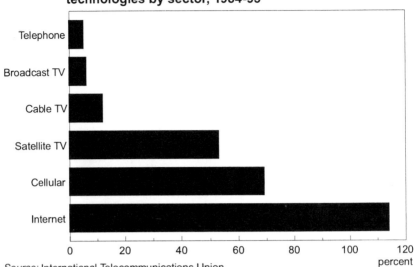

Source: International Telecommunications Union.

Traditional services are experiencing modest growth when compared with new services, such as those specializing in Internet access, call-back services, wireless and mobile services (i.e., low earth orbiting satellites, or LEOS,[2] and wireless local loops), and cellular telephony (figure 3.1). An important reason is that they provide alternative modes of service delivery to the traditional public telephone operator (PTO) scheme. In fact, most of these technologies have grown well beyond the realm and control of national PTOs and threaten to bypass public networks, rendering many traditional market arrangements obsolete. The most progressive PTOs are making efforts to join the parade. Others are struggling to stop these new, expanding forces from eroding the accustomed benefits of monopoly control.

The policy challenge for the World Trade Organization (WTO) is to ensure that users in all countries have access to the new services from competitive suppliers, thus ensuring low cost and high quality.

The Internet

Easier and more widespread access to the Internet global network is the most significant development in the telecom industry. The Internet's rapid

---

[i.e., by a factor of 1,000], which is comparable to cost improvements in computing technology over the same period."

2. LEOS refers to an array of communications satellites that would permit extensive wireless service. One such effort to date is the Iridium Project, which will consist of 66 LEOS units and provide global telecom coverage for up to 10 million users. The principals are Motorola and a number of international partners.

growt ıant methods of handling network design,
proto and content.

Th ently a network used primarily by the US
acad munity.[3] The Internet has grown over the
yea on of networks and the number of Internet
hos average of 40 percent annually. By early 1996,
the 7 million Internet users (over age 16) in the
Ur alone.

tc npanies underestimated the Internet's ability
h ness. In the words of one analyst, the Internet
r telecom operators "with an obsolete system, of
(ıan the recycle value of the copper in the cables"
ry 1996, 6). Many would consider this an extreme
nternet is mostly limited to data transmission,
main the biggest and most lucrative portion of
vices.

ologies could give the Internet the ability to enter
in a big way. In early 1995, a small software com-
dramatically improved early versions of Internet
group of companies calling themselves NetWatch

e World Dialup (FWD) experimental service project
mputer (PC) users free Internet-based voice commu-
s other companies are starting such PC-to-PC voice

at these developments will have a limited impact on
ow computer usage in many countries and because
ents for computer telephony are extensive—at present,
computers running identical specialized software,
card, and other peripheral equipment. Both users also

---

ually a network of networks. There are now a large number of local-
ed on "servers," computers managed by an Internet service establish-
rally subsidized, designed for researchers and universities to use; others
charge usage fees accordingly. These myriad networks interact through
cols. The "backbone" of the Internet is now made up of dedicated
lines linking switches around the world. Management of the Internet
sisting of working groups of concerned parties informally gathered to
s they arise.

4. The ... ge users incur is the flat-rate user fee for their Internet accounts, currently
as low as $20 to $30 per month.

5. In the United Kingdom, the Firecrest Corporation claims to have won exclusive rights
to voice telephony over the Internet (although clearly the legal parameters of such "rights"
remain to be pinned down in Britain). The service would allow Firecrest users to hold
simultaneous international calls of mobile phone quality but at the price of a local call
(*CommunicationsWeek International*, 27 November 1995, 6; *Wall Street Journal*, 10 November
1995, B7A; *Financial Times*, 11 November 1995, 5).

need to be online at the same time. However, newer technologies could circumvent these restrictions. Companies such as VocalTec and International Discount Telecommunications plan to offer computer-to-phone and phone-to-phone services by mid-1996. Computer-to-phone software will allow a user with a computer to call anyone with a telephone through the public switched telephone network (PSTN). Phone-to-phone software will allow users to route phone calls through Internet service providers; such phone calls would be made directly from one phone to another, without the need for computers.[6] It would be extremely difficult to restrict such communications, since digitized Internet voice traffic is indistinguishable from other data.

US long-distance carriers have responded to the specter of unlimited, free (or almost free) international telephony over the Internet with calls for an ban on such services by the Federal Communications Commission (FCC). The General Counsel of the America's Carriers Telecommunications Associations—which represents US long-distance carriers—argues that "if [Internet telephony] explodes, it could dislocate the entire telephone infrastructure" ("Major Telcos Seek Ban on Net Phones," *Web Review*, 7 March 1996). Internet telephony could have a far greater impact in developing countries because of extremely high rates for long-distance and international services.

The Internet is also affecting networking protocols. The international telecommunications community has been trying for several years to adopt a universal protocol for global networking. The PTOs supported the Open Systems Interconnection (OSI) protocol while Internet supporters pushed for the Transmission Control Protocol/Internet Protocol (TCP/IP) on which it is based. The rapid growth of the Internet made adoption of TCP/IP a fait accompli: the protocol has become widely accepted by large business users and even by traditional PTOs.[7] This is not an issue that needs to concern the WTO, for the market has already issued its verdict. But the WTO does need to be concerned that Internet servers based in Singapore, for example, can sign up subscribers in Japan, and vice versa.

The Internet is inspiring large OECD-based PTOs to build regional and global Internet Protocol (IP) "backbones," which can accommodate the

---

6. For computer-to-phone and phone-to-phone communications, both users' Internet service providers require an Internet Phone Telephony Gateway using dialogic computer telephony cards. While voice quality is currently not high with such service, improvements are inevitable in the near future (*Web Review*, 11 March 1996).

7. A survey of 400 corporations found that OSI was being used by 2 percent of their networks and TCP/IP by 25 percent of the surveyed firms (cited in Drake and Frazer 1996, 16). Telia, Sweden's PTO, announced in 1995 that it will use the Internet Protocol as a key technology embedded in its core infrastructure. Telecom Finland is experimenting with a voice-over-IP service, and Deutsche Telekom is considering a national Internet phone system (*IEEE Spectrum*, January 1996, 36).

worldwide needs of their users. In early 1996, Global One (an alliance between Deutsche Telekom, France Telecom, and Sprint) announced that it would build an IP backbone covering 22 countries in Europe, Asia, and North America. British Telecom and MCI have unveiled a similar project to build and connect high-speed Internet backbone networks across Europe and Asia. AT&T and Unisource are finalizing plans for similar ventures (*CommunicationsWeek International*, 19 February 1996, 1). AT&T's decision to close its Network Notes service, which was designed to run on private communications networks, signals the importance that carriers assign to the Internet. A vice president of AT&T recently stated that he was "very proud of this decision because it shows that AT&T is committed to the Internet" (*New York Times*, 29 February 1996, C4). Further mainstreaming of the Internet—and AT&T's commitment to it—is evidenced by the company's February 1996 announcement of five hours of free Internet access monthly for all customers for a year.

The Internet model also challenges the traditional international accounting and settlements regime. The current "accounting rate system" suppresses traffic and keeps charges to end users artificially high—working as a money machine for monopoly PTOs (which explains why the system is still in place).[8] Proposed alternatives to the accounting rate system, such as nondiscriminatory termination charges and sender-keeps-all systems, have been labeled infeasible by monopoly PTOs. However, the success of the Internet demonstrates that a sender-keeps-all system can work.[9] Some analysts even argue that sender-keeps-all is simpler and cheaper to administer (Drake and Frazer 1996, 14). However, many PTOs will likely cling to the existing accounting rate system until WTO negotiations create viable competition that compels the introduction of new arrangements.

Lastly, by charging extremely low flat monthly rates, the Internet has exposed the huge gap between PTO costs and charges. A recent study argues that "the call cost, in direct network charges per minute in September 1994 from the UK to the US, was of the order of 10 cents US while the charge was of the order of 60 cents US, a 500 percent margin. This implies a wide degree of repricing is possible in a free market, especially as costs fall to 10 percent of today's costs" (Forge 1995, 7). WTO negotiations that open the door for new competitors, market by market and country by country, will drive prices toward cost.

Call-Back Services

The gap between PTO costs and rates for competitive international telecommunications services has spawned "call-back" services. Introduced

---

8. For further discussion of the accounting rate system, see chapter 4.

9. The Internet service provider (e.g., America Online or Delphi) collects revenue from its subscribers. There is no revenue split with destination providers, which may be different companies.

in 1990, call-back systems work by routing calls through another "mediating" country (generally the United States), and calls are charged as if they originated in the mediating country.[10] Call-back services cut by half or more the long-distance and international service charges users pay in some PTO-dominated markets and thereby uncover the arbitrarily high prices in that segment of the market. Consequently, these services prod domestic incumbent operators to move prices closer to cost.

Call-back services' revenues are growing 65 percent per year. By 1995, there were approximately 100 US call-back companies, with combined revenues of approximately $500 million.[11] Call-back services have captured large shares of many developing-country markets. For example, Teleintar, Argentina's international services operator, has lost more than 30 percent of the international service market to call-back operators (*Communications Week International*, 2 October 1995, 10).

PTOs in developing countries have attempted to restrict call-back services through court decisions (the Philippines), government orders (China), or tariff reductions (Argentina). However, constant innovation makes it difficult for PTOs and regulators to block call-back services. Uganda, for example, blocked all calls to Seattle, where most major US call-back operators are located. The call-back operators responded by simply rerouting calls through different locations in the United States. When other countries disabled the touch-tone beeps used for call-back services, the services responded by installing voice recognition systems (*The Economist*, 6 January 1996, 67).

In early 1995, several countries complained to the FCC about the "illegal presence" of many American call-back services in their countries. After an investigation, the FCC decided to allow call-back operators to continue their overseas ventures. The FCC subsequently altered its position and allowed call-back operators to serve only those overseas markets where they have not been banned by national laws. However, the FCC will only take action when national enforcement efforts have failed and when the complaining country has documented its enforcement problems to the FCC. At the same time, the FCC regards call-back services as an important proliberalization force and has made clear that it thinks most forms of the service are legitimate price arbitrage.[12] Thus, although the future of

---

10. Under call-back services, a customer dials a designated number in the United States and hangs up after one or two rings. A computer from the US call-back company immediately calls the customer with a dial tone. The customer can then call anywhere in the world using telephone switches belonging to the US call-back service.

11. The market is forecast to grow to $1 billion by the end of 1996 ("FCC Gives the Thumbs Up to Call-Back Services," *Latin American Telecom Review* 4, no. 8, 15 August 1995).

12. In taking steps to limit the provision of call-back service, despite its own view that call-back services represent legitimate price arbitrage, the FCC is observing the wishes of foreign governments under the international legal doctrine of comity.

Table 3.1 Mobile telecommunications market forecasts, 1991-92

Forecast	Organization	Actual outcome to date
Worldwide rate of growth in cellular market	15 percent per year (Economic Services)	Between 1991 and 1995 worldwide growth average was 48.8 percent per year
Cellular subscribers worldwide by 2000	100 million (Motorola)	Approximately 75 million plus by end 1995
GSM subscribers in Europe by 1995	1.9 million (BIS Strategic Decisions)	7 million by mid-1995
Cellular subscribers in Europe by 2000	11.5 million (EMCI) 16 million (ETCO) 20 million (PA Consulting)	Already 19 million plus cellular subscribers in Europe by mid-1995

GSM = Global System for Mobile Communications

Source: Adapted from Kelly (1996).

call-back services is undefined, it is clear that they have prompted competition in international services in many countries.

The role of call-back will diminish considerably if domestic operators dramatically cut their prices. However, the de facto competition generated by call-back service operators can only defeat monopoly prices in limited market segments. Call-back cannot result in a general opening of markets worldwide—for example, it cannot ensure high-quality data transmission or reduce domestic long-distance rates worldwide. In short, this new technology cannot substitute for genuine domestic competition instituted through regulatory reform.

Wireless and Mobile Services

Mobile and fixed wireless services have grown much faster than expected. Growth forecasts in the early 1990s substantially underestimated the diffusion potential of mobile telecommunications (table 3.1). Cellular services grew from 7.3 million subscribers worldwide in 1989 to an estimated 77.9 million in 1995. Many analysts expect that mobile and wireless networks will become full-fledged competitors with traditional wire-line networks, allowing them to bypass the PSTN. Current forecasts by major equipment suppliers and international analysts (based on current percentage growth rates) estimate that the global cellular market will reach between 250 million and 350 million subscribers by 2000—that is, greater than the expected number of Internet users, though for less powerful services (Kelly 1996).

Mobile and wireless services have tremendous potential for challenging traditional PTOs. Cellular networks, for instance, have grown most rapidly in developing countries where wire-line networks are scarce and basic telephone services expensive. In 1994, cellular subscribers in Cambodia and Thailand constituted 60 and 20 percent, respectively, of all telecommunications users. In the Philippines, there were five cellular operators, and the monthly service charge for cellular services was less than half the cost of wire-line telephone service. Cellular subscriptions are now roughly equal to 25 percent of wire-line customers.

Cellular systems are moving to connect with the Internet and provide a link that will further bypass PTOs. Motorola has a new service that converts electronic mail to voice messages, allowing users to check text messages by cellular phone. The system can send and receive faxes and is expected to include voice-to-text translating capacity by 1997. Finland's Nokia has a "smart phone" that approaches the same service in a slightly different way: it flips open to reveal a miniature key board and screen (*Wall Street Journal*, 25 March 1996, B10).

Mobile personal satellite services (MSS) based on low earth orbit satellites (LEOS) could also have a major impact on the telecommunications industry. With compact handsets that can track LEOS, MSS users could connect with wire-line, fixed wireless, and mobile networks anywhere in the world. LEOS can bypass (and thus marginalize) public networks by providing global services to major customers at relatively low cost. Studies related to the Iridium project estimate that the planned satellite infrastructure could ultimately provide unlimited voice communication worldwide at a flat rate of approximately $120 a year.[13] In its initial stages, the Iridium network will have a capacity of about 10 million users and will provide point-to-point connections at $3 per minute anywhere in the world. Other LEOS developers are promising still lower prices.

New wireless local loop (WLL) services are also being embraced by operators worldwide because they offer a low-cost, quickly deployed alternative to traditional wire-line networks. Telecom Finland and UK-based Ionica launched services early in 1996, and Sri Lanka has awarded WLL contracts to Bell Canada and Sweden's Telia. Northern Telecom has built wireless local loops in Vietnam, and the Dominican Republic has had wireless local loops since 1991.

---

13. The Iridium project is a $3.4 billion joint venture of Motorola and other telecom firms. Motorola has a 27.25 percent share. Among the other investors are BCE Mobile Communications (Canada), Sprint (United States), Nippon Iridium Corp. (a consortium of 18 Japanese investors including Sony, Mitsubishi, Mitsui, and Kyocera), STET (Italy), Veba (Germany), and Korea Mobile Telecom. The ambitious project would launch a network of 66 low-orbit satellites and provide universal access via small handheld terminals. Major competitors to Iridium include Inmarsat's Project 21, in which British Telecom and Japan's KDD participate; Globalstar, developed by Loral and Qualcomm; ARIES (Constellation Communications Inc.); and Odyssey (TRW/Teleglobe).

Multimedia

It appears that widely touted multimedia projects, such as video on demand, may not become significant in the near future. Multimedia projects have attracted new players to the telecom arena, such as Walt Disney, Sony, and Microsoft. But for now, the technical difficulties are great, and commercial payoffs seem distant. By contrast, new technologies embodied in the Internet and mobile and wireless technologies are booming, and dramatic growth in these sectors should continue for at least another decade.

The Changing Face of Service Provision

As the foregoing has made clear, traditional forms of ownership and market structure in the telecom industry are fundamentally changing. State-owned monopolies are fast becoming relics. Joint ventures, strategic alliances, foreign companies in domestic markets, plus new players from the entertainment and financial world are restructuring the once-staid industry.

Changes in business organization reflect a combination of new technology, new approaches to regulation, and a new appreciation of global liberalization. The upshot is more competition, but often the competitors are rival groups rather than individual companies. In fact, individual companies may compete in one market and be allies in another. The slow growth of basic telecommunications in the OECD countries has prompted several big carriers to pursue the rapidly growing basic telecom markets of developing countries, often in alliance with local PTOs.[14] Meanwhile, in advanced services, new developments in communications and computing, coupled with fairly open high-end markets in most countries, are inspiring companies to form cooperative ventures.

The changes in the industry have driven companies out of their traditional service niches into new markets. The expansion of corporations and cooperative alliances across the globe and across traditional market boundaries poses serious competitive challenges to service providers in domestic markets. Under the threat of new entrants, local firms are scrambling to form alliances with other local firms in different segments of the communications industry or with foreign companies that bring new capital or expertise.

---

14. Between 1984 and 1994, the compound annual growth rate of main lines per hundred inhabitants was 15.1 percent in low-income countries, 6.4 percent in lower middle-income countries, 6.5 percent in upper middle-income countries, and 2.7 percent in high-income countries. Over the past five years, the growth gap has become even wider, since network growth has slowed in OECD nations during the 1990s while skyrocketing in most developing nations (ITU 1995c).

Many international joint ventures, with new players from the financial world, were created by the privatization of PTOs in developing countries. Privatization in Argentina, for example, gave rise to one of the first international alliances between foreign carriers and financial institutions. The privatized PTO was acquired by two international consortia. Citibank, Telefonica de España, and Techint purchased the company that operates in southern Argentina,[15] while France Cable et Radio, Societa Finanziaria Telefonica (STET), Compañía Naviera Perez Companc, and J. P. Morgan purchased the company that serves the northern region.[16] Similarly, Mexican privatization created a consortium between the Mexican retail and financial conglomerate, Grupo Carso, and two foreign carriers, Southwestern Bell and France Cable et Radio.[17] Privatization in Venezuela and several other developing nations triggered similar joint ventures.

Greater competition in developing-country telecom markets has also led to joint ventures and alliances. A good example is Mexico, where forthcoming competition in basic services has spawned numerous joint ventures, including GTE-TLD-Bancomer, Bell Atlantic-Iusacell, Sprint-Telmex, MCI-Banacci, AT&T-Alfa, and Teleglobe-Westel-IXS-Beep (Ibarra 1996).

Some developing-country companies—especially in the Asia-Pacific region—have even launched their own overseas alliances. Thailand's Shinawatra Computers and Communications Group, for instance, has telecommunications ventures in the Philippines, India, Cambodia, Laos, and Vietnam.

Meanwhile, the major international carriers are forming alliances to provide worldwide telecommunications services. These alliances are aimed at retaining large multinational customers. The new companies offer services such as international toll-free calling, "country direct," calling cards, virtual private networks, closed user groups, messaging, and data transport. Major alliances include Unisource (Telia, PTT Telecom NV, Swiss PTT, and Telefonica), Uniworld (Unisource and AT&T), Concert

---

15. In 1990 (the year of the privatization), Citibank was one of Argentina's main international creditors and headed the Committee of Argentine Creditors. The Spanish government owned over 30 percent of Telefonica de España; the rest was held by small domestic investors and foreign investors. Techint is an Italian multinational corporation with a strong presence in the Argentine market.

16. In 1990, France Cable et Radio was the international branch of state-owned France Telecom. STET (Societa Finanziaria Telefonica) was the Italian telecom provider, partially owned by IRI (Institute for Industrial Reconstruction). Compañía Naviera Pérez Companc was one of Argentina's most powerful economic conglomerates. J. P. Morgan was a major creditor of the Argentine foreign debt.

17. In 1990, Grupo Carso was the sixth largest economic conglomerate in Mexico, with operations in mining, copper manufacturing, auto parts, paper products, retailing, insurance, stock brokerage, food, and tourism. Southwestern Bell was one of the regional Bell operating companies (RBOCs) that emerged as a consequence of AT&T divestiture.

(British Telecom and MCI), and Global One (Deutsche Telecom, France Telecom, and Sprint). AT&T has also entered an alliance in Asia with Singapore Telecom and Japan's KDD (figure 3.2). Facilities-based carriers such as LDDS Worldcom, PanAmSat, and Orion Atlantic have launched global operations to compete with established PTOs. They provide international frame relay, switched voice, wholesale and retail, point-to-point, and point-to-multipoint satellite circuits to customers such as Citicorp, Dow Jones, Bloomberg, and Colgate in as many as 200 countries (*CommunicationsWeek International*, 4 September 1995, 23). A similar phenomenon is occurring in global submarine cable networks, with FLAG and Africa ONE completing a privately sponsored global network.

Telecom companies are also entering new areas, such as multimedia and information services. Telecom providers such as Sprint have formed partnerships with cable TV and wireless/mobile companies such as TCI, Comcast, and Cox. Nynex has joined forces with Viacom; BellSouth, Ameritech, GTE, and SBC Communications have entered a partnership with Walt Disney, while AT&T is trying to diversify its portfolio by building strategic alliances with firms such as Paramount and Silicon Graphics. These rapidly growing global ventures are challenging smaller PTOs in developing economies, especially for the business of multinational corporations.[18]

Several analysts question whether these global alliances might lead to the formation of global cartels and eventually stifle competition. Alliances between large firms might indeed hurt the business prospects of backward PTOs in newly liberalized markets. But it is another question entirely whether these alliances stifle competition.[19] Telecommunications experts believe that "the sheer number of players, the rapidly-changing technology, and the highly-differentiated and changing services make it unlikely that the many contacts that these firms have with one another will have anticompetitive consequences" (Crandall 1996, 26).

This view seems justified, but the impact of changing business arrangements will play out differently in different markets. Joint ventures between dominant local carriers and telecom giants may impede free-for-all competition in some markets. But the question must be asked: compared with what? When compared with existing monopoly arrangements, the new arrangements appear more likely to enhance competition. Home-country

18. For an account of the challenges of telecom globalization to domestic policymaking, see OECD (1995c).

19. Such concerns were raised by the announcement of a merger between SBC (originally Southwestern Bell) and Pacific Telesis in April 1996. The two—both created in the AT&T breakup—would form the second largest telecom firm in the United States. Is the merger in the public interest? The answer to this question depends upon whether the merger produces scale economies and new technologies that result in lower prices or only reinforces the existing market power of SBC and Pacific Telesis.

Figure 3.2 Selected alliances in communications services [a]

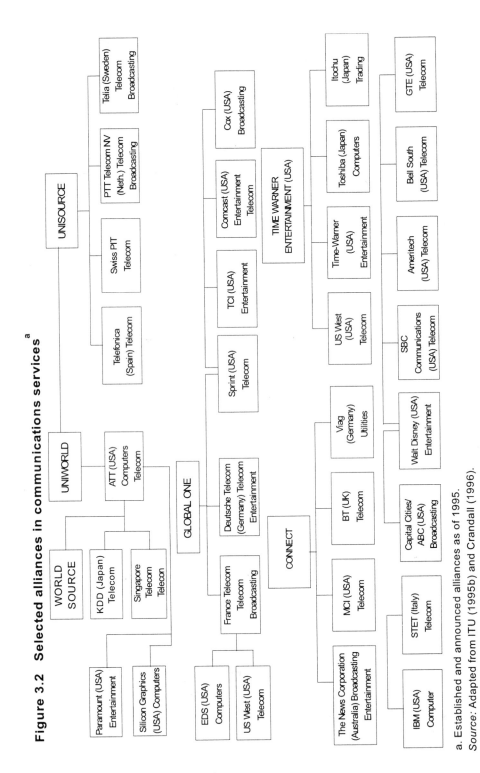

a. Established and announced alliances as of 1995.
Source: Adapted from ITU (1995b) and Crandall (1996).

regulators in the United States, Europe, and many other countries continue to guard against cartel formation. If today's joint ventures should become tomorrow's cartels, then new regulatory initiatives under WTO auspices may be required. For now, the main challenge is to unwind the grip of local PTO monopolies—not to fret about the possible emergence of global cartels.

After decades of debate, the impact of foreign capital on host countries remains an unsettled question. In the telecom sector, studies of the Canadian experience have found no negative economic impact on local economies from foreign ownership, nor any compromise of host-government social objectives (Globerman 1995). Studies of Mexico and Argentina suggest the opposite may be true (Tandon and Abdala 1992). Neither of these studies, however, uncovered a basis upon which to make valid generalizations from a single national experience. In any case, it is probably fair to say that the impact of investment depends more on the terms under which ownership is exercised—whether the market is fully competitive, partly competitive, or still monopolized—than the source of capital.

Conclusion

The mid-1990s represent a turning point in the development of the telecommunications industry worldwide. The long-awaited convergence of telecommunications, computing, and broadcasting is rapidly becoming a reality. But it is not taking the path that many analysts and corporate executives predicted only a couple of years ago. Telephone companies are not jumping into the turf of cable television (CATV) companies, nor are CATV firms providing telephone services to the masses. Video on demand has been tried, with very poor results, while home shopping, home banking, and other information services are rapidly migrating from the proprietary domain of telephone, CATV, and on-line service companies to the realm of rapidly growing open public networks. Most predictions have been proved wrong, and many unexpected developments have occurred.

Some nations are already taking bold regulatory steps to position themselves to take advantage of the new telecom landscape. In early 1996 the United States enacted sweeping new laws permitting new competition among AT&T, regional and local phone companies, cable television firms, and others. The procompetitive regulatory role of the FCC will be enhanced by the legislation, which is already shaping new alliances and strategies in the US marketplace.

A variety of new and advanced technologies have emerged and are spreading worldwide at a staggering pace. The Internet, call-back services, and mobile and wireless telecom services—such as the forthcoming low earth orbit satellites (LEOS) and wireless local loop (WLL)—are among the most important. All of these services operate on different platforms and transmit through various media, but they have several things in common: they provide telecom services at much lower costs than traditional wire-line telephony, they have in most cases developed beyond the realm and control of government-controlled common carriers, they can bypass the public switched network and the control of incumbent carriers, and they provide services that are very difficult to shut down without negative effects on operators and the public in general.

The transformation of the industry is also having an impact at the corporate level, with the formation of many global and national alliances and mergers that are changing the face of service provision. The largest international telecom providers have established global alliances. Yet, the growing complexity of the industry and the pace of its transformation seem to offer safeguards against the possible creation of international cartels.

4

The Benefits of Liberalization

Many national governments have embraced telecommunications liberalization in recent years. Two factors have motivated this trend. The first is the realization that modern telecommunications spur economic growth and attract foreign investment. The second factor is the recognition that under the new technological and economic realities of the telecom industry, monopoly telecom firms, controlled or tolerated by the government, fail to provide the anticipated benefits of universal service and low prices.

This chapter examines the experience of countries that have liberalized telecommunications and draws lessons about the beneficial impact of telecommunications liberalization on teledensity (that is, the number of phones per hundred households), the price and quality of service, and network modernization. To sharpen the analysis, liberalization policies are simplified into two broad categories: privatization of national telecommunications providers and the introduction of competition through measures such as the removal of legal and regulatory entry barriers.[1] While for economic reasons privatization is likely to flow from the introduction of competition, the opposite is not a given. This observation is important, because—as this chapter indicates—competition can generate significantly greater liberalization gains than privatization alone. In considering the policy issues that the World Trade Organization (WTO) can address, this point should be kept in mind.

---

1. In practice, of course, there is a spectrum of policy alternatives because privatization and competition can be sequenced in different ways.

Figure 4.1 OECD international telephone price baskets,[a] January 1992

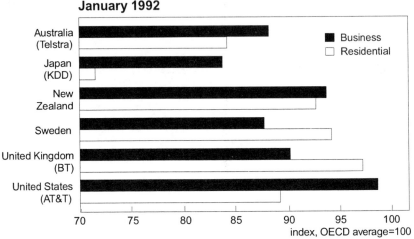

a. The OECD international telephone basket uses price data for the first three minutes of a four-minute direct-dial call. The basket is based on indices that represent the cost of making the same calls in the opposite direction, averaged out over all 24 member countries and weighted by the population size of the terminating country. The business user's basket is weighted assuming that 75 percent of total calls are made in peak hours, and the rest in off-peak, with assumptions reversed for the residential users' basket. Tax is included in the residential users' basket but excluded from the business users' basket where recoverable (OECD 1995b, 37).

Prices

Telecommunications liberalization has had mixed effects on the price of services. The introduction of competition almost always leads to lower rates, sometimes much lower. On the other hand, privatization by itself sometimes leads to higher rates, especially for local service that was usually provided at subsidized rates by the government public telephone operator (PTO).

Developed economies that have allowed competition into the telecom markets have benefited from rate cuts. The underlying reasons are straightforward: the marginal costs of telecommunications per minute of service are very low, and new telecom capacity has been created well ahead of rapidly growing demand. Competitive forces thus work to lower prices.

In the OECD, prices for international services among member countries with international facilities competition are on average 11 percent lower than the OECD mean level (figure 4.1). The experience of the United States and Japan, which have had competition in some telecom sectors for years, suggests that price reductions are large and sustained. The 1984 separation of AT&T from the seven "baby Bell" local service providers, coupled with the entry of competition in US long-distance markets, have exerted tremendous downward pressure on US prices. AT&T's long-distance prices fell more than 70 percent in real terms between 1983, the year before the breakup, and 1991. In Japan, NTT's prices for long-distance services dropped by 50 percent from 1985 to 1992, as a result of an opening to competition in 1986 (OECD 1995b).[2]

In developing countries, competition in basic services is in its early stages, but there is already strong evidence that competition is leading to lower prices.[3] Chile is probably the best example. From 1989 to 1994, due to privatization and the introduction of limited competition, local rates dropped by an average of 36 percent, long-distance rates by 38 percent, and international rates by 46 percent. Full competition was allowed in international services in late 1993. A year later, seven companies were aggressively marketing services at substantially reduced prices. International rates dropped by up to 70 percent in one year, giving Chile some of the lowest international service prices in the world. By late 1995, the price of a call from Chile to the United States was about four times lower than the price of a call from neighboring Brazil to the United States and about seven times lower than from Argentina. Similarly, in China, the launching of cellular services by Unicom—the second operator allowed to provide basic services in the domestic market—prompted the Ministry of Posts and Telecommunications (MPT) to slash its cellular service rates by 30 percent. In Ghana, competition in cellular services led the former monopoly provider, Mobitel, to cut connection charges by 50 percent.

Unlike competition, privatization in developing countries has often been associated with rate increases. In Mexico, for example, the price of local service went up a staggering 1,056 percent in early 1990 due to Telmex privatization. Similarly, in Argentina rates rose an average of 258 percent in the year prior to privatization as the company was "prepped" for sale. In both cases, the increases can be largely explained by government attempts to boost revenues, attract qualified private operators, and improve the chance of a successful privatization. In several cases, high

2. The price NTT charged for a domestic three-minute call from Tokyo to Osaka (daytime) dropped from ¥400 to ¥180 from April 1985 to October 1993, a 55 percent reduction. A three-minute international call from Tokyo to the United States (KDD) fell from ¥1,530 to ¥600 by December 1994, a 61 percent drop. Finally, a leased NTT circuit from Tokyo to Osaka fell from ¥1,100,000 in April 1985 to ¥345,000 by February 1994, a 69 percent drop in price. In each of these cases, the PTO price cut coincided with even lower prices from new carriers in these markets.

NTT was also partially privatized, but the government is still the controlling shareholder. The main change in Japanese telecommunications is competition, not privatization. See Null and Rosenbluth (1995) on poor price performance in Japan due to restrictive regulation.

3. Statistical data and case studies on developing countries are largely based on Petrazzini and Clark (1996b) and Petrazzini (1995).

tariffs also became a means of financing rapid telecom expansion and an upgrade of the national telecom infrastructure.

Economic theory indicates that the nature of ownership (private or public) does not necessarily lead to higher or lower rates. The reason for rate increases following privatization is that governments often subsidize the local rates charged by state-owned operators. With the subsidies gone, rates increase, and if the privatized firm is still a monopoly, the increase can be considerable.

Telecom liberalization by high-rate countries could also help resolve the problem of growing imbalances in international telecom settlements. For many decades, the international settlements system was based on an agreement by PTOs in the International Telecommunications Union (ITU) to use high accounting rates on international calls for cross-subsidizing telecom infrastructure development.[4] Accounting rates are the rates paid by the originating carrier to the destination carrier per minute of outgoing calls. In recent years, many countries have liberalized telecommunications and competitive telecom firms have slashed their collection rates—that is, the rates charged to the public. But many countries have not liberalized, and in these nations dominant PTOs still charge high collection rates. These collection-rate differences in turn create huge differences in the flow of traffic between pairs of countries and thus big imbalances in international settlements. Countries with low collection rates have seen their outbound traffic surge and their settlement deficits soar, given the high level of accounting rates. The problem exists primarily between developed and developing countries: in 1994, 70 percent of all US net settlement payments—approximately $3 billion—were made to less-developed countries (LDCs).

The standard defense of high accounting rates is that developing countries can use the revenues gathered under the current framework to improve their telecommunications systems. However, there is little evidence that countries customarily use these revenues for building infrastructure. All too often, revenues are diverted to political and social goals that do nothing to increase telephone penetration.[5] In Egypt, for example, a portion of the revenues from the telecom operator—ARENTO—are being used to finance construction of the Metro System.

A study by Henry Ergas (1996, 14) finds that "holding other structural factors constant, investment per main line is negatively related to the level of nominal and effective rates: in other words, countries which are

---

4. For details on the history and workings of the international telecommunications settlement regime, see, for example, Frieden (1993) and Ergas and Paterson (1991).

5. For example, in 1987 Telmex contributed $500 million to the Mexican National Treasury but received only $150 million for operations and network development. Dirección General de Telecommunicaciones, the other Mexican state-owned operator, contributed $100 million to the Treasury and only received $30 million.

expanding their networks most rapidly tend to have significantly lower (rather than higher) nominal and effective accounting rates." Ergas concludes that many governments use high accounting rates to impose a hidden tax on domestic and foreign consumers, but choose not to invest these revenues in telecom infrastructure development.

In any event, high collection rates are an unattractive strategy for financing telecom expansion and modernization because they undermine the competitiveness of many firms positioned in various sectors throughout the country. High communications costs discourage operations and trade beyond the limited geographical area in which a company begins its operations. When potential markets are located far from home, high international and long-distance communications costs can impose a hidden toll on competitiveness.

Whatever the merits of their arguments, high collection rate countries generally want to retain the current system of high accounting rates and protect their high domestic revenues and international settlements income. However, the system is already under attack. Developed nations facing increasing settlement deficits are pushing for reform. The US Federal Communications Commission (FCC) is leading the charge (Aamoth 1995).

In a recent policy statement, the FCC proposed different accounting rate policies for countries with different degrees of liberalization. In competitive markets, the FCC encourages US carriers to explore alternatives to accounting rates, including end-to-end service by a single supplier and nondiscriminatory termination charges. In high-rate countries, the agency has indicated that it may support US carriers that refuse to pay high accounting rates after existing agreements expire (FCC 1996, 9). In a recent case involving Argentina, the FCC in fact directed all US carriers to deposit their payment of accounting rates into an escrow account, to be withheld from Argentina until fair termination charges are levied on all foreign carriers. The Argentine PTO subsequently unveiled changes that led to a resumption of accounting rate payments.

Other institutional supporters of change include the ITU (the institution that created the current system) and national carriers such as Sweden's Telia. The ITU has recommended moving toward cost-oriented and nondiscriminatory accounting rates. And Telia is pushing some European providers to abandon accounting rates and base their international rates on low national interconnection rates. This revolutionary approach could reduce inflated accounting rates by as much as 80 percent (*Communications Week International*, 19 February 1996, 9).

The settlements system is also increasingly besieged by technological changes. Some developing countries, such as Argentina and Hong Kong, have admitted call-back services into their domestic markets to stimulate competition. Call-back service prices are so much cheaper than PTO prices that in Argentina, for example, they are used not only for international calls but also for domestic long-distance calls. The national monopoly carrier charges $2.84 per minute for a domestic long-distance call outside an 800-kilometer radius. The same call, routed via a call-back operator thousands of miles away through the United States, costs less than half as much—$1.39 per minute.

Since call-back services are considered outgoing calls from the country in which the call-back operator is located (e.g., the United States), they have a two-fold impact on developing countries. Under the existing accounting rate system, LDCs earn more settlement revenue, but their PTOs also lose revenue because they handle less international traffic. Most studies have found that incumbent carriers in high-rate countries lose more revenue through lost traffic than they gain through increased settlements income (Aamoth 1995; Frieden 1996; "Callback Contributes to Economic Development," *CommunicationsWeek International*, 9 April 1996).

In Brazil, for example, while the incumbent international carrier charges $2.59 per minute for a call to the United States, call-back operators offer the same service for $0.79. Prior to call-back services, Brazil's Embratel would get 78 percent of the $2.59 charged per minute, and the US carrier got the rest. According to one US call-back operator, in a call-back transaction carried out of Brazil, Embratel now makes only 22 percent of what it once did in an international direct-dial call, while the call-back operator gets 5 percent, and a local representative earns 3 percent of the per minute charge. Thus, the customer pockets savings of 70 percent of what he would have paid for the call.[6] Not surprisingly, monopoly PTOs are fighting to keep call-back services out. In countries that have admitted them, incumbent carriers have lowered their international rates.

Some telecom analysts, such as Robert Aamoth (1995, 10), counter the arguments for accounting rate reform by pointing out that the costs facing the average LDC carrier are more than twice those facing the average developed-country provider. Aamoth favors different accounting rates for developed and developing countries. He argues that settlement imbalances are caused not only by accounting rate imbalances but also by "country direct" services offered by US carriers in overseas markets.

Country direct service refers to a variety of collect-call services. US customers in overseas locations, for example, get a direct connection to their US carrier, which puts them through to a desired number. The call is charged to a US account as if it originated in the United States. Therefore, the calls appear in the accounting settlement as having originated in the United States. Country direct services accounted for approximately 40 percent of the US settlement deficit during 1992 (Aamoth 1995, 11). How-

---

6. For further details on the impact of call-back services on accounting rates, see Frieden (1996), Aamoth (1995), and "Callback Contributes to Economic Development," *Communications Week International*, 9 April 1996.

ever, all this statistic really says is that country direct—a cheap way of making overseas calls—encourages traffic volume.

Other new products are changing the calculus of the accounting rate debate as well. In September 1994, the FCC opened the way for "international simple resale" between the United States and the United Kingdom. This regime permits leased international lines to attain unfettered access to the public networks in both countries, bypassing the accounting rate system altogether. Canada is now open to this regime as well.

Universal Service

The impact of telecom liberalization on universal service (the provision of telecommunications services to all households and small firms) is tremendously important, since the achievement of universal service is the most common argument used to defend monopolistic telecom companies. A common belief is that profit-maximizing private firms will not find it worthwhile to serve smaller towns, rural areas, and poorer households because those users cannot generate sufficient revenue to pay for the requisite infrastructure.

Recent evidence from a growing number of developing countries strongly contradicts this belief. Liberalization (whether in the form of competition or privatization) does not hinder the pursuit of universal service; instead, it actually boosts network penetration and the availability of services to the population. In part, this is because countries that allow private investors in the telecom arena may require specific performance obligations such as "build-out" in rural areas—expanding main lines to reach a fixed punctuation target.

Developing countries that privatized their telecom sectors have seen their networks expand more quickly than those that remained under state monopoly. This is particularly true in Latin America and Asia, where teledensity in countries with privatized telecommunications grew twice as fast during the five years following privatization compared with countries that did not privatize (Petrazzini and Clark 1996a). A similar contrast between privatized and nonprivatized systems among least-developed nations in the Pacific Basin and Africa also shows that those under private ownership achieved much faster teledensity growth than their state-owned counterparts (ITU 1995a, 25).

Few developing countries have experienced competition in basic wire-line services for any length of time. But competition in cellular services has existed for longer periods, making this a fruitful area to test the impact of competition on teledensity.[7]

---

7. The effects of liberalization on teledensity in developing countries are set forth in Petrazzini and Clark (1996a).

**Figure 4.2   Asia and Latin America: cellular teledensity under
competitive and monopoly markets, 1991-94**

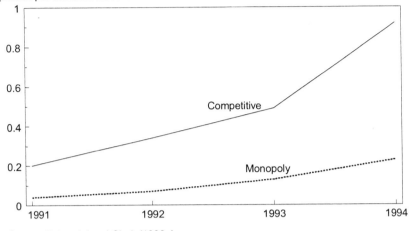

phones per hundred households

Source: Petrazzini and Clark (1996a).

A comparison of competitive and noncompetitive cellular markets in Asia and Latin America clearly shows that competitive cellular markets have achieved much higher network penetration than monopoly cellular markets (figure 4.2).[8] This gap becomes more pronounced over time. It is also noteworthy that competition in cellular telecommunications exerted a positive impact on teledensity in wire-line services. Even though the two services are not perfect substitutes, competition in the cellular market apparently inspired PTOs to improve their performance. In many developing countries, the scarcity of wire-line networks and the length of waiting lists for service have made cellular service attractive, especially to the large-business users that generate the bulk of PTO revenues. The possibility of losing these clients helps propel PTOs toward reform.

In general, anticipated competition appears to have had as profound an impact on monopoly carriers in developing countries as actual competition. In fact, several countries have specified precise schedules for introducing competition in monopoly telecom markets. The expectation of competition has spurred monopoly providers to significantly increase the number of main lines added each year. However, this effect is only detectable when the onset of competition is less than three years away.

The best example of this phenomenon is the Philippines, where the announcement of competition in 1993 inspired the incumbent, Philippine

---

8. The study also tested other possible variables affecting cellular teledensity growth (such as GDP levels, GDP growth over time, and country specific factors) and found that none of them was as important in explaining teledensity growth as competition (Petrazzini and Clark 1996a).

Figure 4.3 Lines added in OECD countries: competitive versus noncompetitive markets, 1990-94

1990=100

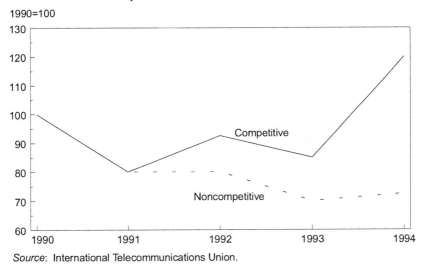

Source: International Telecommunications Union.

Long Distance Telephone company (PLDT), to launch a Zero Backlog Program, emphasizing measures such as rapid network expansion. Since the program was launched, main-line installation has skyrocketed from an annual average of 19,625 main lines between 1985 to 1992 to an unprecedented 224,500 lines a year between 1993 and 1994.

Similar lessons can be drawn from the experiences of developed countries. An analysis of the 25 OECD member economies found that provision of new lines in competitive countries outpaced that in closed nations, growing 21 percent from 1990 to 1994 in countries with competitive telecom markets, while installation of new lines dropped by 28 percent in countries with noncompetitive markets (figure 4.3). The United Kingdom and Japan illustrate this same point. Both countries liberalized their markets in the early 1980s and saw network penetration rise from 31 percent in the United Kingdom and 35 percent in Japan to 49 percent and 48 percent, respectively, by the mid-1990s.

Japan was among the first countries to launch a public cellular service in 1979, but competition was highly restricted until 1994, when two new firms were allowed to participate in the market. As a result, rules preventing customers from buying their handsets were dropped, differentiated rate structures were introduced, prices fell considerably, and the number of subscribers doubled within a year. The Scandinavian countries, on the other hand, started cellular service at a similar time but had a fairly competitive environment from the outset. As a result, Sweden had the highest cellular teledensity in the world by 1994, with 15.8 cellular subscribers per 100 people, while Japan, even after doubling its teledensity, had achieved only 3.5 subscribers per 100 people.

Historical experience in the United States supports the hypothesis that competition promotes teledensity (Mueller 1993, 1996). In the early 1890s, the Bell system served only the 72 most prosperous cities in the country, providing virtually no service to the rural areas; teledensity growth was less than 1 percent per year. Between the mid-1890s and early 1920s, widespread competition sharply increased telephone penetration, and by 1910 teledensity growth was over 18 percent per year.[9] Network deployment by independent companies in the rural areas of the United States was so successful that, by the end of the competitive era, in the early 1920s, a higher percentage of farm families had telephone service than nonfarm families. In Europe, where no competition was allowed, teledensity growth remained between 1 and 2 percent until the 1920s.

In sum, one can conclude that there is little evidence that competition hinders universal service. On the contrary, most of the available data point to a rapid increase in the installation of main lines under competition—leading to the fulfillment of universal service goals.

Service and Network Quality

Experience in recent years indicates that firms in liberalized telecom markets modernize their networks faster than firms in nonliberalized markets. Liberalized markets also provide higher quality service, though so far this trend is evident only in developed countries.

Liberalization clearly promotes network modernization. Countries with competitive or privatized environments in Latin America, for instance, have enjoyed much higher levels of digitization than Latin American countries with public monopolies (figure 4.4).[10] In Asia, the Philippines had fewer digital main lines in the early 1990s (7 percent) than Myanmar (18 percent).[11] However, the Philippines began to liberalize its telecom industry in 1993, while Myanmar continued to protect its traditional PTO.

---

9. Mueller (1993, 353) argues that "the universality of the telephone network became an issue at that time because the competing systems were not interconnected with each other. A competitive race between unconnected telephone systems ensued, a phenomenon which I label 'access competition'."

10. Small countries, and countries with underdeveloped networks, can reach high levels of digitization in a very short time through modest investments and network upgrades. Comparing countries that have small or new networks with those that have larger or older networks can bias the analysis. For that reason, the analysis here concentrates on selected countries with comparable network development and size.

11. ITU studies also find a positive correlation between digitization and market liberalization in the OECD area (see ITU 1995b, 115).

Figure 4.4 Digitization in selected Latin American markets, 1988-94

percent digital main lines

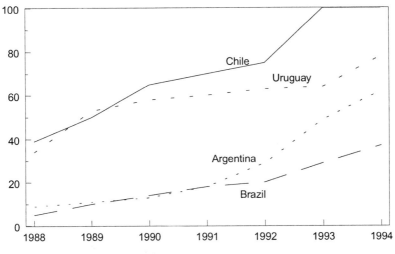

Source: International Telecommunications Union.

By 1994, the Philippines' digitization level had reached 64 percent, while Myanmar's was only 35 percent.

The positive effect of liberalization on service quality is apparent in developed countries, where universal-service goals have largely been achieved (everyone who wants a telephone gets a telephone), and operators have shifted their attention to issues of service quality. Within the OECD, liberalized markets have reached higher service-quality standards than nonliberalized ones—whether measured by the number of faults cleared by the next working day, the number of unsuccessful local calls, or the number of faults per 100 main lines. The FCC has quantified some advantages OECD countries with competitive telecom systems have over those with noncompetitive systems (Pepper 1995):

- 97 percent reduction in waiting time to get telecom service;

- 17 percent lower call failure rate;

- 39 percent fewer faults per 100 lines;

- 34 percent lead in number of phones digitized.

Developing countries, on the other hand, have concentrated on extending their networks and fulfilling universal-service goals rather than on improving quality. As a result, the principal impact on service quality so far has been a dramatic reduction in waiting time to get telephone service for new subscribers and quicker clearance of faults throughout the system.

Data from national administrations, however, at this point show no clear, generalizable correlation between liberalization and service quality in developing countries.

Economywide Benefits

Improvements in the telecommunications sector also have economywide benefits, which can be categorized in four types: faster economic growth, better response to basic needs, cost savings, and attraction of foreign investment.

Economic Growth

A cross-sectional econometric study of the 50 US states found that telecommunications development favorably encourages economic growth. In fact, high-quality telecommunications may have a more significant impact on growth than other infrastructure inputs such as education, energy, and highways (Dhalokia and Harlam 1994).[12] The impact of giving a remote village its first telephone line is much greater than the impact of adding another line in a big city. Indeed, a study of 60 nations found that the impact of telecommunications on economic development was greatest for countries with low teledensity (Hardy 1980). Since most people in developing countries live in rural areas, this point is of tremendous importance.

This finding should not be surprising: communications and the transfer of information is crucial to economic activity. High-cost, low-quality telecom services can block the rise of communication-dependent economic activity such as the transmission of data or faxes. A comparison of the costs of some of these activities using conventional and digital network technology is shown in figure 4.5. Indeed, as policymakers from different nations try to foster environments that attract good jobs, they have increasingly come to recognize that an advanced telecom infrastructure is a critical ally for achieving their goals.

Basic Needs

While a growing telecom sector boosts economic growth, it confers the greatest benefits on a country's least-developed sectors. Low-cost telecom services can help poor regions cater to basic human needs such as health and education.

---

12. For an extended literature review on the macroeconomic benefits of telecommunications and an excellent evaluation of the methodologies used, see Saunders, Warford, and Wellenius (1994, chapters 4 and 5). Also see Cronin et al. (1991, 1993).

Figure 4.5 Comparative costs of typical file transfer tasks using ISDN and conventional telephone lines, 1993

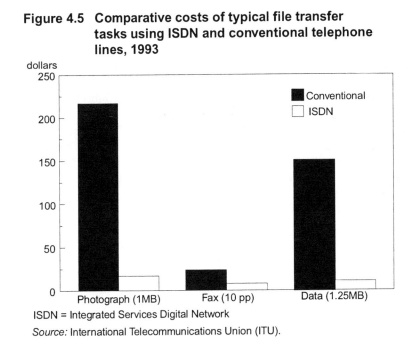

dollars

Conventional
ISDN

Photograph (1MB)   Fax (10 pp)   Data (1.25MB)

ISDN = Integrated Services Digital Network

Source: International Telecommunications Union (ITU).

Pioneering work in the remotely located Pacific island nations provides a model. A mid-1990s effort to implement a telemedicine and telehealth network between Hawaii and several Pacific island nations found that the marginal cost to the system for adding primary care services, specialty consultations, and education programs amounted to only $5,000. Project leaders found that "one of the major barriers to extending telemedicine and telehealth applications throughout the Pacific Islands Region is the state and cost of the telecommunications and information infrastructure" (Bice et al. 1996, 654).

In countries such as the United States, where competition in domestic telecommunications has sharply cut the price of telecom services, a variety of telemedicine initiatives are being implemented. From Melbourne, Florida, the Harris Corporation has set up a link with the Medical Center at the University of California-Los Angeles (UCLA) located 3,000 miles away. Radiologists and other doctors from UCLA help support medical diagnosis and treatment at the Florida medical center. The system not only lets Harris employees get services they would otherwise not receive, it also saves the company $2 million a year in medical expenses (*Business Insurance,* 20 February 1995, 3). Other studies in the United States have found that the use of telecommunications to deliver medical services could cut the nation's health care bill by as much as $36 billion. Telemedicine projects in Montana, Iowa, and Georgia seem to confirm this prediction ("Long Distance Medicine," *Business Health,* June 1994).

At the international level, an educational audioconferencing network between the University of the South Pacific's Fiji campus and other Pacific island nations has been highly successful. The system generated savings in travel costs that are at least 10 times the cost of using the network (Hudson 1994, 349).

An innovative way of catering to basic social and commercial needs in developing nations is through the establishment of Community Teleservice Centers (CTSC), or telecottages. From a technological point of view, CTSCs are an advanced version of public call offices. They bring together, in a public office, computers, modems, printers, fax machines, video equipment, and telephones. From a social and economic point of view, the initiative provides a center for education, business training, and cultural activities (Goussal 1996; Qvortrup 1989).

Both international organizations and national governments have endorsed CTSC initiatives. The ITU's first World Telecommunications Development Conference, held in Buenos Aires, embraced CTSCs as one its main initiatives related to the Integrated Rural Development (IRD) plan. Brazil has launched a national plan to create approximately 3,000 CTSCs across the country by the year 2004. One of the Brazilian CTSC projects is located in Toledo, a community of 86,220 in the state of Parana. By October 1995 the Toledo Center was serving 13,775 customers a month—a 54 percent increase over the average of the previous 25 months. But the immense benefits of these applications will remain illusory unless telecom prices in most countries drop closer to the real cost of providing the service. CTSCs need cheap telecom services in order to flourish. This example underscores the important role the WTO negotiations can play in extending the gains from telecom technology to a broader, and in many cases needier, population.

Cost Savings

Telecommunications services can also generate significant savings by cutting costs and promoting economic efficiency. In Uganda, for example, an estimated 250 worker-years of skilled government labor are wasted every year on approximately 40,000 administrative trips that could be handled by telephone (Saunders, Warford, and Wellenius 1994, 26). A study in Yemen found that 10 to 25 percent of all transportation could be avoided if good and reliable telecommunications were available (Richter 1995). Research on rural satellite networks in Peru estimated that each telephone call produced an average savings of $7.30, compared with alternative means of communication (cited in Hudson 1995). In Singapore, the adoption of telematics in the public sector has produced tangible benefits. It is estimated that every dollar spent on the project has yielded three dollars in returns. The quality of public services has risen dramatically, and labor costs have decreased significantly as public-sector employment has decreased from 9 to 6 percent of the national work force (Nair 1995, 70).

Foreign Investment

A developed telecommunications infrastructure also plays a key role in attracting foreign investment—an important consideration for many developing countries.

The rise of the software-industry in Bangalore, India, is probably among the best examples of the positive impacts of low-cost, reliable international communications (Hanna 1993; Harindranath and Liebenau 1995). The industry had export revenues of $300 million in 1994 and expects to employ 100,000 people in 1996. More than 150 of the 600 firms in Bangalore operate on global contracts only. None of this would have been possible without telecom networks that allow firms in Bangalore to work with parent companies thousands of miles away (Petrazzini and Harindranath 1996).[13] Much of the software industry's growth is related to liberalization in the Indian computer industry, but limitations in telecom infrastructure could constrain future growth.

Other nations suffering from high unemployment, such as Ireland, have begun to explore the potential of global telecommunications networking as a means of bringing jobs to the country. US health care company CIGNA has set up back-office operations in the Irish village of Laughrea. The center handles approximately 20 percent of CIGNA's transactions, which are processed and sent back to the United States through leased lines (Forge 1995, 39). Similarly, Singapore Airlines now carries out many back-office operations in Shanghai.

Conclusion

Since the turn of the century, state-owned monopoly was viewed as the market structure most likely to provide cheap, universal service. Yet after decades of supporting telecom monopolies, most nations are still far from achieving universal service. In recent years, new market arrangements that emphasize competition and private participation in the telecom sector have proved to be powerful policy tools for extending networks and increasing teledensity. Countries that have allowed competition and/or privatized their national carriers have experienced much faster network

---

13. Low-cost, highly skilled, English-speaking workers are also an important component of India's software industry success. Yet none of these factors would make a difference if the international telecom infrastructure was not in place.

growth than those that have remained under traditional state-owned monopoly schemes. Similarly, countries that opened their markets to foreign firms have experienced sharp improvements in the quality of services and network modernization compared with those still operating under restricted-entry regimes.

In developing nations, privatization by itself has generally led to price increases—mostly in local services. But the introduction of competition in both OECD and developing nations has brought prices down for all services. Nevertheless, in most nations the rates for long-distance and international calls still remain high. Technological and institutional pressures are eroding the current international accounting rate regime. With a push from the WTO, the end of the era of PTO monopolies and the demise of accounting rates will lead to big reductions in long-distance and international rates worldwide.

Improvements in telecom services exert strong positive effects on domestic and international economies. Studies across a large number of cases and over extended periods show that better, cheaper telecom services lead to faster economic growth, significant efficiency gains and cost savings, and better conditions for attracting foreign investments and selling into foreign markets. The availability of telecom services at affordable prices in developing nations can also significantly improve the delivery of education and health services, among other basic needs.

In sum, adopting competitive market arrangements, mainly through the lowering of entry barriers to competition within a WTO framework, should slash rates, realize the goal of universal telecom service, and spur economic growth.

5

The Costs of Liberalization

Because the liberalization of telecom services is relatively new, most countries extrapolate their experience in other downsized industries to gauge the prospective costs of telecom liberalization. This has led to the erroneous conclusion that liberalization inevitably hurts at least two sets of actors: employees and the dominant public telephone operators (PTOs).

A growing volume of evidence, however, shows that the damaging effects of liberalization on employment and dominant PTOs are not nearly as dramatic as expected. In fact, in many cases, there is enough evidence to turn conventional wisdom on its head. Competition has often had a positive, rather than negative, impact on employment in the broadly defined telecommunications sector.

Employment

Fears of increased unemployment in the dominant PTO are generally a great source of resistance to telecom liberalization in countries that have not yet experienced liberalization. The perception that competition creates unemployment is bolstered by the extensive press coverage of industry layoffs, such as AT&T's recent announcement of 40,000 job cuts over the next few years.[1] Job creation—less dramatic, but often more significant— does not get nearly as much attention.[2]

---

1. The number of AT&T workers to be involuntarily laid off will be much lower than the initially announced figure of 40,000. Some of these workers will find jobs in other parts of AT&T, and many others took the company's buyout offer. AT&T's latest estimate is that about 18,000 workers will have to leave the firm involuntarily over the next three years.

2. For instance, India's Department of Telecommunications and China's Ministry of Posts

Isolated anecdotes lack an overall, long-term perspective and do not separate the effects of competition from those of technological innovation and other changes. More systematic studies suggest that telecom liberalization does not hurt employment; it creates jobs. A study of OECD telecom markets, for example, found that employment cuts resulted more from factors such as market saturation and technological innovation than from telecom liberalization. The study revealed that, contrary to conventional wisdom, competitive telecom markets have actually created jobs in the broad telecom sector, to a significant degree offsetting the effects of market saturation and technological innovation (OECD 1995a). Studies of developing countries have found similar trends. Competitive telecom markets have usually generated employment growth, while the work force in monopoly markets has generally decreased (Petrazzini and Clark 1996a).

In fact, competition appears to have played a decisive role in creating telecom jobs in OECD economies (OECD 1995a, 1995b). These countries already have extensive telecom networks, so building new network facilities can no longer play the traditional role of employment generator. Moreover, the digitization of networks has decreased the number of employees needed for network maintenance. But competitive telecom markets have created jobs in such areas as marketing, sales, customer service, software design, and systems analysis. While overall employment has fallen in the OECD countries, competition has sparked a movement away from lower-skilled jobs linked to network construction toward higher-skilled jobs associated with market and software development. Whether employment increases or decreases has much to do with how competitive the sector is overall.

In the United States, AT&T and the regional Bell operating companies (RBOCs) have steadily shed workers since the breakup of AT&T. What is less well-known is that overall employment in the competitive long-distance market has been growing (figures 5.1 and 5.2). Evidence suggests that OECD countries with traditional PTOs, unlike the United States, are not creating telecom jobs as quickly as they are losing traditional jobs (OECD 1995a).

Moreover, most developing countries have maintained their telecom employment levels. But countries with competitive markets have increased employment levels more than countries with monopoly PTOs. Unlike OECD countries, developing countries have relatively undeveloped public switched networks. Whereas developed countries had an average teledensity of 52 lines per 100 people in 1994, developing countries had an average of only 5 lines per 100 people. Low teledensity levels

---

and Telecommunications together created more than 100,000 jobs during the last five years through sectoral reform and growth. Similarly, MCI and Sprint have added nearly as many jobs in the United States as have been lost.

Figure 5.1   Employment in monopoly US telecommunications markets, 1988-92

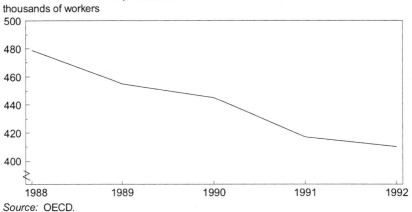

thousands of workers

Source: OECD.

Figure 5.2   Employment in competitive US telecommunications markets, 1988-93

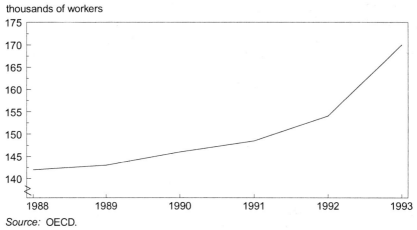

thousands of workers

Source: OECD.

require massive "catch-up" investment in fixed networks and the deployment of substitute services, such as mobile networks. Thus, about 71 percent of telecom investment in developing countries goes to build wireline and mobile networks. Since these activities are labor-intensive, developing countries have little problem maintaining telecom employment levels.

A recent study of 26 Latin American and Asian countries found that average employment has expanded rather than declined over the last five years (Petrazzini and Clark 1996a). As in OECD markets, competition boosted employment levels. Markets with competition were the only ones that consistently increased employment levels, while two-thirds of the monopoly countries saw their work force shrink during the same period, often considerably. Overall, competitive markets increased employment by 16 percent, while privatized monopolies decreased employment by 9 percent.

In India, where a new telecom policy has brought competition to several market segments, the incumbent operator, the Department of Telecommunications, plans to expand its work force over the coming years. In the face of competition, the agency has improved its marketing and opened thousands of public call offices (PCOs) around India. Based on this expansion strategy, the agency expects PCO employment to increase from the current 700,000 to as much as 3 million in the year 2000.

Other factors, such as GDP growth or network modernization, do not appear to have affected employment as much as competition. The cited study found that GDP grew on average by 6 percent in Asian countries over the last five years and telecom employment increased by 9 percent. In Latin America, GDP grew on average by 4 percent, but telecom employment *fell* by 10 percent. The main difference between Asia and Latin America was the extent of competition, not the rate of GDP growth.

The experience of developed countries suggests that network modernization probably eliminated jobs in developing nations, just as in OECD countries. However, this trend was overshadowed by the tremendous job creation associated with network installation and service expansion associated with liberalization.

A related employment point is that new market segments create jobs, even as labor opportunities shrink in traditional sectors. For instance, NTT's work force in traditionai telecom services was trimmed by 16 percent between 1990 and 1993, but mobile and data communications services employment grew by 33 and 21 percent, respectively, between 1992 and 1994. The Japanese Ministry of Posts and Telecommunications estimates that, since the introduction of domestic market liberalization, employment in the infocommunication sector has grown faster than employment in all other domestic industries. In the United States, jobs related to the public switched telephone network declined by 10 percent between 1987 and 1994, while jobs in the mobile and cable TV sectors expanded by 10 percent over the same period.

In absolute terms, in the OECD nations taken together the number of jobs created by new telecom industries does not currently equal the number lost from the traditional telecom sector. This reflects the significant decline in expansion of the traditional telecom network and the slow rise of nontraditional services in countries that have hesitated to allow competition. But the story is different in developing nations, where expansion of the basic telecom network is the single most important infrastructural undertaking of the late 1990s. In these nations, absolute telecom sector employment is poised to expand markedly.

Figure 5.3 Employment trends in mobile services in Australia, 1990-94

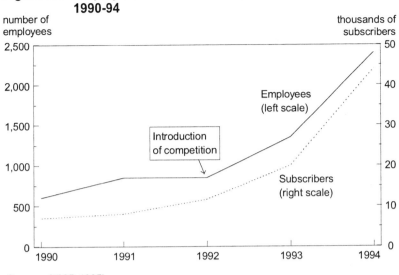

Source: OECD 1995b.

Competition has been a major force in increasing market size and creating employment in the new telecom sectors, both in the OECD countries and in developing nations. The experience of Australia and India are illustrative. The introduction of competition in the Australian mobile services market led to a rapid increase in the number of cellular subscribers, which in turn increased employment in the sector (figure 5.3). In India, where cellular service was recently launched, new mobile operators are hiring staff at a frenetic pace. The Birla-AT&T group alone plans to hire more than 5,000 employees in the next three years. Considering that the group is only one of more than thirty mobile operators licensed in the country, the number of jobs created by the new, competitive mobile market may exceed 100,000.

Employment generation by nontraditional operators is usually underestimated because, among other things, small, private telecom networks are often left out of published data sources. By 1993 there were 700,000 private networks in the United States and 14,000 in Europe. These networks probably generated considerable numbers of jobs but were generally not counted by the traditional data collection mechanisms of the telecommunications industry (OECD 1995a, 24).

Impact on PTOs

PTOs have strongly opposed telecommunications liberalization, both because they want to protect their monopoly rights and because they see themselves as potential victims of cutthroat competition. Recent evidence from countries that have liberalized their markets shows, however, that even under the pressure from procompetitive regulators, former monopolies have retained most of their customers. In competitive markets, prices and profit margins have fallen considerably, but the customer base has not deserted wholesale.

Market Share

The experience of liberalized markets shows that PTOs are not as vulnerable as they once feared. In fact, most new entrants have failed to grab significant market shares, let alone threaten the dominant PTO.

The OECD countries provide excellent case studies, based upon their long experience with competition. In Britain, for example, British Telecom (BT) holds an unchallenged hegemony in both local and long-distance markets after several years of competition. In 1994, six years after competition was introduced in the local market, BT still served 40 times more customers than its competitors. After 10 years of competition in long-distance services, BT still controls over 90 percent of the market. In the United States, AT&T still controls roughly 58 percent of the long-distance market, despite 10 years of aggressive price competition from MCI and Sprint.

Developing countries provide similar evidence, though their experience with competition is relatively short. In China, the 1993 authorization of China United Telecommunications (China Unicom, or Lian Tong in Chinese) was greeted with anxiety by China's Ministry of Posts and Telecommunications (MPT), the dominant PTO. Operating as a joint venture between the Ministry of Electronics, the Ministry of Railways, the Ministry of Electric Power, and several large state enterprises, China Unicom already had significant networks in place. Unicom planned to carry 10 percent of China's long-distance calls and 30 percent of its mobile calls by 2000 and was supported by a high-profile marketing campaign. Conventional wisdom held that the company would soon become a major contender in the Chinese market. Two years after it was launched, however, the company faced severe obstacles in establishing its market presence, raising financial support, and in acquiring the necessary technology. By late 1995, Unicom was only offering mobile services in four cities.[3]

In China, the dominant PTO retained power in large part through an array of anticompetitive practices designed to thwart China Unicom. Inadequate interconnection oversight and weak monitoring and enforcement mechanisms allow dominant PTOs to retain their control in many

---

3. Two months after operations were launched, there were only 400 subscribers in the Beijing Unicom mobile network.

telecom markets. This is still too common a story. The Philippines had competition for several decades, but by 1993 the Philippines Long Distance Telephone (PLDT) company still controlled about 86 percent of the market, due to a lack of interconnection-rights enforcement. In Mexico, extremely high interconnection rates precluded competition in the local market for years. In other words, the absence of effective regulation of interconnection rights simply allows a monopoly PTO to charge exceptionally high if not exorbitant rates to access the network.

Some countries have shown that proper regulatory mechanisms can allow new entrants to capture significant market share. Chile's multicarrier system, which operates in the long-distance and international markets, allowed new competitors to capture 16 percent of the Chilean international service market within seven months of entry.[4] With proper, procompetitive regulatory oversight, the established PTO may not be decimated, but it will definitely lose some customers. Without question, it will also have to slash prices and improve service to remain in business.

Revenues and Profits

Telecom liberalization has exerted a mixed impact on PTO revenues and profits. The mixture depends on the emphasis—privatization or competition. Privatized companies that maintained their monopoly positions have increased their profits substantially. On the other hand, competition has significantly trimmed profits for most companies in the market, with gains usually going to consumers.

Privatization in several developing countries led to steep rate increases, which afforded generous revenues to privatized monopolies.[5] In Argentina, Telefonica de Argentina and Telecom Argentina earned estimated rates of return over fixed assets ranging from 25 to 32 percent during the first year after privatization.[6] Foreign companies have generally found their operations in Mexico and Argentina more profitable than their home-country operations. Southwestern Bell's profits on its Telmex investment in 1991, for example, exceeded profits from all its US operations. Telefonica de Argentina's 1994 profits were 30 percent higher than those of Telefonica de España, its Spanish parent company.

While privatization alone sometimes leads to lower prices and smaller profits, competition—with or without privatization—almost always lowers both prices and profits. Newcomers fare poorly in initial years because

---

4. The multicarrier system is a mechanism by which users can access any carrier at any time by dialing a code before the desired number.

5. For a discussion of why privatization is often accompanied by rate increases, see chapter 3.

6. Telefonica de Argentina is a subsidiary of Telefonica de España. Telecom Argentina is a consortium of France Telecom, the Italian firm STET, and national investors.

of the industry's high fixed costs and pronounced economies of scale. Newcomers in the Chilean and the Philippine markets incurred first-year losses ranging from $2 million (Globe Telecom GMCR in the Philippines) to $12 million (Bell South Communications in Chile). The performance of dominant PTOs in newly competitive markets can also be lackluster. For example, severe competition in the Chilean market hurt former long-distance carrier Empresa Nacional de Telecomunicaciones (Entel, with first-year losses of $16.5 million) and CTC-Mundo (first-year losses of $8.8 million).

The longer experience of developed countries with competition (relative to developing nations) suggests that while profits may decline immediately after competition is introduced, they will usually increase with larger revenues in the medium term. In the first burst of competition, intensive investment by newcomers, corporate restructuring by the dominant PTO, and price wars all combine to lower profits throughout the industry. But profits usually improve as carriers become more efficient and as lower rates lead to increased demand for telecom services. New Zealand Telecom, for example, enjoyed a cumulative annual revenue growth of 5 percent in the five years following the introduction of competition. The revenues of NTT and British Telecom grew by a cumulative average of 4 percent between 1986 and 1993.

Much of the concern about the effects of liberalization on PTOs has focused on the likely impact generated by the licensing of new service providers in domestic markets. Over the next decade, call-back services, Internet data and voice services, global operations by large carriers, and low earth orbit satellite (LEOS) services will confront PTOs whether they like it or not. The real question for government policy in developing countries is not "whether to liberalize" but "when to liberalize" (see also ITU 1995a, 63 and 89; OECD 1995c; Petrazzini and Clark 1996a). Those countries that stay out of the bargain at the World Trade Organization (WTO) and try to protect their dominant PTO for another 5 or 10 years will simply enter the 21st century with a carrier and a system far behind the frontier of telecommunications. The result will be self-imposed, second-class telecom citizenship.

Conclusion

The social cost of policy change has always been an integral part of debate on economic transformation. Job losses are generally associated with reforms that aim at increasing efficiency and productivity, such as the introduction of competition. This is probably true in the case of stagnant and declining industries, but the assumption does not apply to booming sectors of the economy, such as the communications industry. In OECD nations taken as a whole, for example, the number of telecommunications employees has declined in recent years, but this trend seems more closely related to technological innovations than to market structure. In fact, monopoly markets have consistently lost workers, while competitive markets have experienced an overall gain in the number of employees. The same is true for developing countries, where competitive markets maintained or increased their labor force rather than slashing the work force as once feared. On the other hand, monopoly companies in developing nations have on average reduced their work force.

The impact of liberalization on PTOs has been mixed. Privatization has generally been associated with an extension of the monopoly and therefore with considerable economic gains for the incoming operators. Competition instead has shrunk profit margins in the sector, and during the early stages of liberalization both incumbent and new carriers have generally incurred losses. The longer experience of OECD countries suggests, however, that profit margins stabilize in the medium term.

6

Key Negotiating Objectives

This chapter summarizes the key issues addressed by the Negotiating Group on Basic Telecommunications (NGBT) and still under debate within the World Trade Organization (WTO). Several of the issues have already been raised. The emphasis here is on the most important questions.

Competition and Privatization

Liberalization encompasses both the introduction of competition (measures to open telecom markets to alternative service providers) and privatization (the sale of public telephone operators, or PTOs, to private investors). Liberalization, particularly through competition but also through privatization, can attract capital and improve technology and managerial expertise.[1] The difference between competition and privatization has been emphasized throughout this study. These terms are often too casually paired; their effects can be dramatically different.

Competition lowers prices and improves quality more dependably than privatization. This is because public telecom operators are often subsidized, and with privatization those subsidies are typically eliminated. The result can be higher rates for basic services, a hike that can be severe. Without competition, privatized monopolies tend to focus on protecting their profit margins at the expense of improving the range and quality

---

1. Privatization usually attracts foreign investment. Arguments in favor of foreign investment can be found in McCormack (1980) and Todaro (1981). Arguments against are summarized by Lichtensztejn (1990) and Moran (1986).

of service. Furthermore, they may suppress new technologies that might compete with their core hardwire business. Cellular service is particularly likely to be neglected. Procompetitive regulation is usually required to avoid the halfway outcome: a privatized, more efficient monopoly.

In countries with monopoly PTOs, telecommunications remains one of the few money-making state enterprises. But just as one compares a firm to its competitors when appraising performance, one must view PTO profits in the context of alternative market structures. It is clear that moderately profitable state-owned telecom providers entail a high social cost in terms of unmet demand for services and quality improvements, lost efficiency gains, and failure to provide advanced infrastructure. Further, they do not even assure the overall job growth that can be expected of a truly competitive telecom sector. Once this context is understood, it becomes apparent that competition is a more powerful tool for lowering prices, improving quality, and gleaning the attendant benefits (jobs and investment) than privatization alone.[2]

The International Telecommunications Union (ITU) offers "compromise solutions" for countries that are not ready to open basic services to international competition. One such strategy would allow domestic competition between carriers in which foreign firms hold a minority of shares. These joint ventures could attract capital, technology, and expertise while strengthening domestic carriers instead of challenging them while they are relatively underdeveloped (ITU 1996).

India is experimenting with such an arrangement. Its Department of Telecommunications has not been privatized, but local services and "intracircle" long-distance services have been opened to competition. The country has been divided into 20 telecom zones, and in each of them the national carrier will compete in basic wire-line services with a private company in which foreigners are allowed to own up to 49 percent of shares (and may control management). In cellular services, licenses have been granted only to private (local or foreign) operators to offer services on a duopoly basis. The policy has shaken up the national carrier, which has rapidly responded to the challenges with new business and market strategies. It has also set the basis for the development of domestic private telecom firms. And it has managed to attract significant foreign capital, technology, and expertise.

Regulatory Reform

Telecom liberalization is ineffective without regulation to prevent anti-competitive behavior. The dominant PTO will try every possible engineer-

---

2. This is particularly true if privatization goes hand in hand with a monopoly concession. While such transactions bring funds to the government treasury, they are one-time deals, which if not adequately regulated can result in undesirable side effects: a rise in prices,

ing, financial, and legal trick to thwart new entrants. Only effective regulation can block the natural responses of entrenched monopolists.

Only one developed nation (New Zealand) has replaced telecom regulatory agencies with broad competition legislation covering all facets of the economy. This approach will seldom work in developing countries. Most developing nations lack a culture of competition, laws that prevent collusion, and essential enforcement mechanisms, such as a strong, independent judicial system. Regulators specific to the telecom industry are thus essential.

Building an efficient, effective regulatory agency has proved an elusive task. The process has been particularly arduous in countries that have had little or no regulatory tradition (Wellenius et al. 1993, 10). This section identifies and discusses the key issues related to the regulation of competition in the telecom sector. The analysis focuses on developing countries because they face the greatest difficulties in establishing regulatory agencies.[3]

Autonomy

Private investors, wary of highly politicized processes, have long demanded independent regulators who are removed from government influence.[4] More recently, foreign investors and domestic telecom workers have expressed the same desire.[5] While many governments oppose the transfer of regulatory powers to autonomous agencies, they must reverse their accustomed stance in order to ensure reform.[6]

An independent regulatory agency is particularly important in countries where the government retains any ownership and/or control of domestic telecommunications carriers. In such cases, regulatory agencies are hard-pressed to enforce procompetitive regulations that PTOs do not like, such as fair interconnection, structural and accounting separation,

---

lack of improvement in service quality, and work force reductions. Competition, meanwhile, has lasting positive economic effects such as lower service prices, expanded infrastructure, more diverse and better services, and increased investment.

3. Developed economies, of course, have had their own problems keeping regulatory agencies sufficiently independent from the powerful targets of their work.

4. There are many ways to design regulatory agencies (see, e.g., ITU 1993; Wellenius and Stern 1994, part VII; Nair 1995).

5. India provides a good example of this trend. In the process of granting new licenses to private operators, both private investors and telecom workers demanded an independent regulatory agency to mediate many of the controversial issues that arose during bidding.

6. In Argentina, the Ministry of the Economy fired the entire board of directors of the regulatory agency, the Comision Nacional de Telecomunicaciones, because of "inefficiency." A court ruling overturned the official action because it lacked a legal basis (*Communications-Week Latinoamerica*, Tercer Trimestre 1995). The board was once again fired in March 1996.

cost-based pricing, and technical transparency of the network. Regulators controlled by governments that also own and operate the dominant carriers simply cannot be effective.

Regulatory autonomy involves not only independence from direct government influence but also insulation from the influence of major interest groups, such as operators, equipment suppliers, large businesses, and residential users. In the United States, before the breakup of AT&T, the legitimacy of the Federal Communications Commission's decisions was challenged with arguments that the FCC had been "captured" by the firms it was supposed to regulate.[7] Similar capture problems, real or apparent, exist in many developing countries today.

Some governments might become even more reluctant to devolve their regulatory powers to autonomous agencies in the years ahead, as the boundaries between broadcasting, computing, and telecommunications become blurred. One reason is that the commercial stakes are getting larger. Another is that the merging of technologies makes the control of mass communications more difficult and, in the eyes of some governments, requires greater vigilance. Some governments, for example, fear that the rapid growth of the Internet could promote political opposition, social instability, and cultural imperialism. For this reason, China restricts Internet use and availability.[8] Similarly, information ministers of the Association of Southeast Asian Nations (ASEAN) announced in March 1996 the creation of a regulatory body to oversee the Internet "invasion."[9] The ministers expressed concern about the content made available over the Internet and its potential to spread racial and religious tension within their countries.

Precisely because of these "practical" objections to an open, competitive telecom system, the creation of autonomous, adequately funded regulatory agencies is high on the list of many NGBT participants.

Transparency

In most countries, regulation of the telecom sector is far from transparent. It is often unclear who makes the rules or why such rules come about. Moreover, regulations are susceptible to change with the political wind.

---

7. These arguments provided part of the impetus for the breakup of AT&T. It was alleged that AT&T had become too powerful and had captured the FCC so that regulatory decisions were serving the interests of AT&T rather than those of the general public. These arguments, along with the core concern over "bottleneck facilities," were central in the debate (see Horwitz 1989; Stone 1989).

8. The limited nature of China's current telecom infrastructure provides an uncommon ability to impose such limitations.

9. ASEAN members are Brunei, Indonesia, Malaysia, Philippines, Singapore, Thailand, and Vietnam.

Market liberalization creates pressure for a more transparent, stable regulatory process at both the domestic and the international level.

At the domestic level, increased private participation has led to demands for regulatory transparency and accountability. Many developed and developing countries now require regulators to provide public notice and an opportunity for private parties to debate proposed regulations. To comply with international agreements, however, most countries will need to increase the transparency, precision, and accountability of their telecom regulatory systems.[10]

For example, Article III of the General Agreement on Trade in Services (GATS) and Article IV of the Telecommunications Annex require national regulators to publish rates and other conditions applicable to end users. The GATS contains a provision to protect commercially confidential information, but a country violating the transparency requirements could be subject to the Dispute Settlement Understanding (DSU) process.[11]

The GATS also limits the ability of governments to change regulations on a whim, and the NGBT has sought to reinforce these general constraints in the context of telecommunications. Once commitments are in place, regulators who are bound by WTO agreements cannot easily reverse themselves, since arbitrary changes can be challenged through the DSU process (ITU 1996).[12]

This will be troublesome for some developing countries. Countries with only a nascent comprehension of the complex forces and trends shaping the telecom industry are often anxious about agreements that would limit their future actions. These countries want to retain policy flexibility.[13] However, increased transparency and accountability are also critical factors in attracting private investment (particularly from foreigners), securing reasonable credit ratings, and improving internal long-term planning. Many developing countries are finding that the gains from increased foreign investment outweigh the loss of regulatory discretion.

Human and Financial Resources

Effective telecom regulation is not feasible without skilled professional staff and adequate funding. These are serious problems for many developing countries.

---

10. For an excellent analysis of the impact of WTO telecom negotiations on national regulatory regimes, see ITU (1996).

11. An additional issue related to transparency is the proposal that international accounting rates be published and departures from national treatment be justified. See the section on accounting rates below.

12. Malaysia, for instance, could not recently have reversed previous market-access commitments if these commitments had been made in the context of an NGBT accord ("Asian Regulators Apply Breaks," *CommunicationsWeek International*, 7 October 1995).

13. The NGBT framework can accommodate changes in pricing policy but requires that the core commitment to interconnection principles be locked in.

Money is always short, and the absence of adequate financing can easily undermine the formal institutional autonomy of a regulatory agency. New financing mechanisms such as licensing fees and levies on operator revenues should be explored. However, the goals will be undermined if the treasury collects the funds for discretionary allocation to the regulator or if treasury officials dominate the regulator's budgetary management.

Professional staffing presents a similar challenge to developing nations. Under the old systems, regulators were generally engineers. In the new, market-driven environments, many kinds of professionals are required: engineers, lawyers, accountants, financial analysts, and economists. Many developing nations cannot meet these staffing requirements. International institutions (the WTO, World Bank, and others) can play a supporting role in this regard.

The NGBT accord and other multilateral telecom agreements will set forth regulatory guidelines on issues such as licensing, pricing, interconnection, and standards. The same accords could provide the impetus for improving the professional expertise of regulatory agencies, both by establishing common training in regulatory objectives (for example, under ITU auspices), and by appraising major regulatory decisions (for example, under the WTO's Trade Policy Review Mechanism).

Interconnection

The ability of new operators to connect to the public switched network is crucial to their survival and growth. Ideally, interconnection arrangements should give customers access to the fullest possible range of services, regardless of the carrier they choose. Interconnection agreements work well when two or more carriers have similar market power and they benefit to approximately the same extent from the increased traffic generated by interconnection. This rarely happens. Hence, the larger carrier is tempted to use every available legal, economic, and engineering trick to make interconnection difficult for new carriers. Doubtful means have been employed in many markets. The experience of countries as divergent as the United Kingdom, the United States, New Zealand, the Dominican Republic, Mexico, Australia, and China indicates that regulatory intervention is necessary for ensuring fair interconnection arrangements.

The absence of information or erroneous information about the technical features of the public network, for example, can delay interconnection. Regulatory oversight is essential to ensure that incumbents create a transparent public network architecture and publish information about any technical changes on a timely, procompetitive basis.

Similarly, if the incumbent only offers interconnection at limited points in the network, newcomers may be forced to build extra infrastructure to reach the available points. Alternatively, they may have to send traffic through uneconomical routes. Either solution would put the new firm at a cost disadvantage. Therefore, regulators should require incumbents to allow interconnection at any point of the network and in ways that are compatible with the new carriers' operations. The quality and routing of transmission for competing carriers should be no less favorable than what the incumbent provides to itself.

The argument that such demands unfairly take "property" from the dominant PTO fails to recognize two points: first, the monopoly concession surely gave the dominant PTO enough value in past years to pay for laying the basic network and, second, any fair interconnection rates will pay an appropriate share of the marginal costs of network expansion.[14]

Another question is "symmetry"—that is, whether the dominant PTO can claim the same interconnection rights as those it must grant to new entrants. The precedent set by leading legislation is to enforce symmetry only when new entrants have gained adequate market power.[15]

Because of the complexity and diversity of interconnection agreements, regulators have usually encouraged operators to reach agreements among themselves, based upon guidelines established in law or regulation. This has been the case in countries as different as Mexico, Australia, the United States, and the Dominican Republic. In general, regulators intervene only at the request of one of the parties or when existing agreements seem against the public interest. Given greater diversity at the global level, however, international telecom agreements may require a more interventionist stance.

One plausible strategy for solving many interconnection and competition problems is to require the incumbent to divest its service from its infrastructure operations. Under the new scheme, the public network would come under the control of a company that does not compete for customers but does bulk sale of transmission capacity. This new business would have all the incentives to keep its prices and interconnection conditions as favorable as possible to as many operators as possible because its business would lie in the growing number of service providers and the volume of businesses they generate. On the other side, the incumbent's divested service operations would have to compete on equal terms with other service providers for access to customers, and its business would ultimately rest on the services it provides and not in control over "bottleneck facilities."[16]

---

14. See Graham and Lawrence (1996, 11-12) for a discussion of natural monopolies and services that rely on their networks.

15. When this approach is followed, regulators should determine whether a carrier has achieved adequate market power on a case-by-case basis, using criteria such as degree of customer choice, number of competitors, market shares, ease of market entry, ability to offer new services, and the freedom to offer wholesale prices (OFTEL 1994).

16. There are a number of proposals around this scheme (e.g., Solomon and Walker 1995; Venturelli 1996).

Structural and Accounting Separation

Structural and accounting separations are crucial to development of a transparent competitive market. Structural separation requires a company that provides services in various segments of the market (i.e., basic voice services, value-added services, mobile cellular services, and so on) to create separate subsidiaries with independent administration, accounting, and record keeping operations. In Hong Kong, for example, Hong Kong Telecom has been required to create separate subsidiaries for wire-line operations (HKTC), international service (HKTI), and mobile services (HKT CSL).

Accounting separation requires each company to keep, within its operations, independent accounts for the various commercial transactions related to service provision. In the United Kingdom, for example, British Telecom is required to have a network account (costs and charges to other operators), an access account (costs and charges to customers), and a retail account (costs and charges to subsidiaries). Structural and accounting separations are aimed at avoiding cross-subsidies within the company and other anticompetitive behavior.[17] Cross-subsidies can thwart new firms' entry into the competitive segment of the domestic market.

Number Portability

Number portability is essential for meaningful competition. There are two types of number portability: geographical number portability (when a user moves to a different location and retains the same telephone number) and operator number portability (when a user changes telecom service providers and retains the same telephone number).

Operator number portability is particularly vital to sustain competition. Consumers dislike the hassle and costs associated with changing telephone numbers. Businesses in particular face significant costs when changing numbers, such as advertising the new number. Recent studies show that almost 70 percent of subscribers who would consider switching to a new operator if they could retain their telephone number would not switch if forced to change to a new number (Ovum Ltd. 1994).

Pricing Policy

Pricing policy has generally stretched the resources and imagination of regulators. Finding the right pricing mechanism (usually a choice between

---

17. The adoption of structural and accounting separations is a necessary but not a sufficient condition to ensure a competitive environment. In addition, implementation must be monitored and enforced.

rate of return and price-cap approaches[18]) and the right mix of prices between the various services offered is a regulatory challenge. Market liberalization should ease some of the pressure by letting market forces determine prices. But regulators still need to play an essential role in preventing both monopoly and predatory pricing.

Accounting Rate Reform

Accounting rates are the prices charged by a destination carrier for terminating an international call. Usually, two international carriers terminate calls for each other, and the net amount paid by one or the other is the settlement charge. If the destination carrier is a dominant PTO, it can use its power over the local market to charge high accounting rates to the foreign carriers that originate traffic. Obviously, the accounting rate system was created in an era when nearly every country had a telecom monopoly. In the current era, when some countries have competitive telecom services and others do not, it leads to bizarre results. The most bizarre is that, despite its competitive edge in the telecom arena, the US industry annually pays more than $3 billion in net settlement charges to foreign carriers.

Liberalization of telecom services should lead to reform of the outdated accounting rate system. High accounting rates curtail the use of telecom services. They do this by punishing telecom providers that offer their customers low international collection rates while rewarding operators that charge their customers high international rates. The reason for this odd mix of rewards and punishments is that high collection charges discourage outbound traffic and thus decrease a carrier's settlement charges under the international accounting rate system. By contrast, low collection charges encourage outbound traffic and increase a carrier's settlement charges.[19]

The accounting rate system allows high-rate countries with monopoly PTOs to extract huge rents from low-rate countries with competitive telecom carriers. Not surprisingly, the high-rate countries are less interested in negotiating changes in the current accounting rate regime.

The forces of international competition and technological change are nonetheless propelling reform. Call-back services—by simultaneously taking service revenues away from the PTO in protected, high-rate mar-

---

18. The rate-of-return approaches involve determining a reasonable return on investment to the telecom operator, then setting prices to produce that return. The price-cap approach starts with a desired price structure (often decreasing over time) and permits the operator to attain whatever profitability it can given the price structure.

19. For a discussion of the accounting rate and international settlement systems, see chapter 4.

kets while increasing the accounting rate deficits of competitive countries—are forcing the accounting rate regime to the fore of negotiations. "International simple resale," which was approved by the FCC for service between the United States and the United Kingdom in September 1994, may hasten the demise of the current regime as well. Under this plan, a foreign carrier can lease lines over which to make end-to-end connections, thereby bypassing the accounting rate mechanism altogether.

Several proposals for multilateral agreement on accounting rate reform have been made in the past. The most passive proposals favor a slow reduction in accounting rates toward actual cost. The slow reduction approach defers to many PTOs' concerns: they claim a need for continued high accounting rates to pay for universal service and to grow out of the infant industry status of many of their new business lines. More activist plans for dismantling accounting rates include facilities-based payments, sender-keeps-all approaches, and volume-based payments.[20] The proposal most compatible with the national-treatment principle would be call-termination fees. Under this system, the rate for incoming international traffic should be the same as the rate that domestic firms pay for interconnecting. The ITU recommends this approach.

At the NGBT in March 1996, the United States put forth a proposal that would obligate member countries to publish their accounting rates and would require them to justify international rates that are significantly higher than domestic termination rates. At present, only the United States and the United Kingdom publish their rates. To the extent that the broader goal of ensuring competitive basic telecom services is met, the accounting rate system must eventually become history.

---

20. Under facilities-based payments, the originating operator pays according to the use of facilities provided by the terminating operator. Sender-keeps-all allows the originating operator to keep all the revenue. Under volume-based payments, compensation paid by the sending country is tied to the volume of calls sent on a descending scale (to encourage low collection charges on outgoing traffic).

7

Conclusions

Propelled by a critical mass of technology and managerial innovation, the telecom sector has entered a revolutionary period. Yet more is needed to sustain this revolution: national and international agreement on pro-competitive policies and complementary regulation. Only if this is achieved will the potential of telecom innovations be realized worldwide.

National reform is already taking place—but only in a few places. Overhauls have occurred in the United States, the United Kingdom, Mexico, Chile, New Zealand, and a handful of other nations. In the nations where procompetitive changes have been made, former monopoly PTOs have acquired a new look, promising ventures have sprung into life, and new products and services with tremendous cost savings and quality improvements have followed.

Ensuring reform is not easy. Competition in a domestic telecom market requires a professionally staffed, well-financed, autonomous regulatory agency. Telecom competition cannot flourish without highly specific guidelines and rulings on a variety of issues, such as interconnection, structural and accounting separations, number portability, and pricing policies. Experience worldwide demonstrates that the success of the regulatory process depends on its transparency and public accountability. Common performance objectives for national regulators could be an early milestone for worldwide liberalization.

To achieve goals such as widespread transparency in the regulation of telecom markets, cooperation above the national level is needed. Without parallel international agreements on the principles of competition, the promise of a new telecom era will be enjoyed by comparatively few nations, while others continue to lag far behind. At this juncture, negotiations within the framework of the WTO, in particular within the Negotiating Group on Basic Telecommunications (NGBT), provide the most promising venue for achieving a meaningful international agreement. Born out of the Marrakesh agreement that concluded the Uruguay Round, the NGBT's main goal is an all-encompassing global accord for opening domestic telecom markets both to competition and private investment.

The NGBT aims are based on two indisputable factors: telecom technology and liberalization. The former has changed dramatically in the past decade, yet in many countries market structures and ownership arrangements still need to adjust. The latter—especially through increased competition but also in the form of greater private participation—has proved the best means for delivering the benefits of new technology. For most countries, the question is not whether to liberalize telecom services but how and when to do it. This study highlights two main conclusions: failure to reform has a very high cost for national competitiveness, and competition is more important and desirable than privatization.

The data and analysis presented in this study are part of a growing volume of evidence showing that market liberalization has significant positive effects both for the provision of telecom services and for the performance of national economies. Teledensity in liberalized markets has increased at least twice as fast as in nonliberalized markets, and the difference in telecom penetration appears to be increasing. Prices have come down dramatically in competitive markets, but they have risen (usually for local residential services) in places where privatization has gone hand in hand with an extended period of monopoly. International and long-distance prices remain high in most countries, reflecting the power of dominant PTOs. The dated accounting rate system, which underpins high international rates, will pass into history once telecom competition becomes a global reality.

This study also calls into question a number of entrenched assumptions about the impact of liberalization. Overall telecom employment does not appear to suffer as a consequence of liberalization. While dominant PTOs will likely shed jobs, in competitive markets new branches of telecom activity are creating a large number of jobs, especially in marketing and services. Dominant PTOs have retained a considerable share of the market even after liberalization, but the opening of markets at home and abroad usually erodes the huge profit margins that these firms once enjoyed. Quality of service and network modernization has also sharply improved in developed nations with competition. In developing nations with liberalized markets, the evidence is more anecdotal—digitization in competitive markets has grown much faster than in closed markets, for example—but there is not yet sufficient evidence to draw a clear correlation between liberalization and improved service quality.

Let's Make a Deal

The NGBT talks that ended 30 April 1996 represented a first attempt to reach global agreement on liberalizing telecommunications in its new era. Many of the elements needed to attain a critical mass of commitment on global telecom liberalization were present. Negotiators knew the stakes, the issues, the deadlines, and the process. Yet they still failed to successfully conclude the talks.

The NGBT's failure to meet its deadline raises a long-standing, important question: whether the World Trade Organization (WTO) can deliver results in the context of single-sector negotiations. With many "intrasectoral" trade-offs to be made within the single-sector context of telecom talks, it was hoped that an unconditional most-favored nation (MFN) basis could be achieved through the NGBT. Obviously, the result was not encouraging.

By granting themselves a 10-month extension to reach a deal by February 1997, negotiators kept alive the hope that successful sectoral negotiations can serve as an adjunct to the hefty WTO rounds. But many commentators are already saying that the negotiating structure, not the underlying readiness of the telecom sector for international agreement, is to blame for the failure to reach an early deal. After all, similar failed outcomes have occurred in financial and maritime services. If the NGBT fails a second time, the single-sector negotiation will have to be discarded as a viable approach. At that point, two alternatives will be left: continue single-sector talks but conduct them on a conditional MFN basis—in which only members of the "club" get the benefits of market access according to club rules—or fold the talks into a big-package WTO negotiation.

APPENDICES

Appendix A:
Estimating Telecom Cost Savings and Quality Benefits

Gary C. Hufbauer

Table 1.1 presents a rough estimate of the potential cost savings and the value of quality gains likely to be generated by worldwide telecom market liberalization phased in over 1997-2010. **The terms "cost savings" and "quality gains" refer to benefits that would be enjoyed by business and household users of telecom services. The calculations do *not* include an allowance for the loss of monopoly profits by PTOs.**

Table 1.1 shows the calculated annual gain in 2010 and the cumulative total for the 14 years from 1997 to 2010. The estimated gains are portrayed in two ways: according to national per capita income levels and geographically by region.

Countries that already enjoy significant competition in the telecom sector are excluded from these calculations. For present purposes, these are Canada, Denmark, Finland, New Zealand, Sweden, the United Kingdom, and the United States. However, even these countries would surely see gains as well, resulting from additional external competition in basic and value-added services and from the entry of domestic operators into international markets.

The starting point for these estimates is projected 2010 GNP (expressed in 1993 dollars) for each set of countries. This is extrapolated from 1993 GNP data, assuming 6 percent growth for low-income countries, 4 percent growth for middle-income countries, and 2.5 percent growth for high-income countries. The 6 percent figure for low-income countries may seem generous, but most of the population of these nations is located in China, India, and other nations of East and South Asia. Most of these countries have been growing at rates in excess of 6 percent, and rapid growth seems likely to persist over the next 15 years.

Based on the current experience of noncompetitive telecom countries in the OECD, we assume that telecom revenue would be 2 percent of GNP for all countries in 2010 in the absence of competition and privatization. This is a conservative estimate, since telecom services are growing faster than GNP in nearly all countries.

Cost savings from liberalization reflect lower per-minute rates for domestic and international service, lower monthly fees for basic service, elimination of the accounting rate system, and lower prices for equipment due to scale economies corresponding to greater demand for services. The basic assumptions used to estimate these savings are taken from the observed experience of OECD countries that have liberalized their telecom markets, as compiled by Robert Pepper (1995) based on OECD data:[1]

- cost savings for business users of 18 percent;

- cost savings for household users of 14 percent;

- therefore, simple average cost savings of 16 percent.

The calculated value of quality benefits results from improvements such as a larger range of new services (cellular, pagers, etc.), fewer failed calls, quicker repair of lines and central switches, better access to pay phones, and clearer connections. Based on the experience of competitive and noncompetitive markets in OECD countries (again, from Pepper 1995), the rough order of magnitude of quality gains can be sized up by these statistics:

- increase in cellular telephone density of 118 percent;

- increase in pay phone density of 42 percent;

- decrease in waiting time to get telephone service of 97 percent;

- decrease in call failure rate of 17 percent;

- decrease in faults per 100 lines of 39 percent;

- increase in percent of phones digitalized of 34 percent.

For low-income countries (as categorized by the World Bank), improved service is assumed to be worth 150 percent of calculated cost savings. For middle-income countries, quality benefits are assumed to be 100 percent of calculated cost savings. For high-income countries (excluding the competitive markets listed above), quality benefits are assumed to equal 50

---

1. Data used in these assumptions were compiled by Robert Pepper, "Competition and Reinventing Regulation," Federal Communications Commission, May 1995. Population and GNP data are from the World Bank, *World Bank Development Report 1995.*

percent of calculated cost savings. These are arbitrary figures, but within the ballpark of judgments by telecom experts.

Putting these assumptions together, 16 percent of the telecom portion of 2010 GNP, which is estimated to be 2 percent, equals the cost savings (or, 16% × $GNP2010 × 2%). In addition, in a low-income country, for example, 150 percent of those cost savings represents the assumed value of quality benefits. The two together equal the calculated total gains from telecom liberalization. The gains over the 14-year period from 1997 to 2010 (inclusive) are summed using a straight-line cumulation, starting with zero in 1997 and ending with the full calculated value of cost savings and quality benefits in 2010.

It should be noted that this methodology only shows the static benefits from liberalization. Important additional gains will be derived by firms that expand their scope of operations using better, cheaper telecom services. If these harder-to-estimate figures were added in, the calculated benefits of liberalization would be higher. The estimating method is conservative in other counts as well: for example, in some of the high-income countries in table 1.1, a quality benefit equal to 50 percent of cost savings is probably low. Some of them, notably Japan, will probably enjoy higher quality gains.

It should be emphasized again that this methodology does not purport to measure welfare gains traditionally computed using the deadweight-loss triangles of international trade theory. Rather, the estimates in table 1.1 reflect calculated benefits to business and household users of telecom services, with no deduction either for lost profits by PTOs nor for any decline in supernormal wages or overstaffed payrolls among PTO employees.

As a reality check, consider that 1994 global telecom revenues were approximately $500 billion. Assuming that this figure will grow at 5 percent annually in real terms, telecom revenues in 2010 can be projected at approximately $1.1 trillion. Against this base, the estimate in table 1.1 of gains in 2010 of $149 billion represents user savings of only 13.5 percent. This check suggests that the rough estimates of cost savings and quality benefits in table 1.1 are not unduly optimistic.

Specific Calculations

User Savings Calculations

Low-income countries

1993 population, 3,092 million; GNP per capita, 1993 dollars, $380; total GNP, 1993, $1,175 billion; assumed 6 percent real growth in GNP, 1993–2010 (factor = 2.69), leading to projected GNP in 2010 of $3,161 billion.

- Telecom cost savings in the year 2010, with competition: 16% × $3,161 × 2.0% = $10.12 billion.
- Telecom quality improvement in the year 2010, with competition: $10.12 billion × 1.50 = $15.18 billion.
- Total competition benefits in the year 2010 = $25.30 billion.
- Straight-line cumulation of benefits, over 14 years (1997-2010 inclusive, starting at zero in 1997 and ending at $25.30 billion in 2010): $25.30 billion × 7 = $177 billion.

Middle-income countries

1993 population, 1,596 million; GNP per capita, 1993 dollars, $2,480; total GNP, $3,958 billion; assumed 4 percent real growth in GNP, 1993-2010 (factor = 1.95) leading to projected GNP in 2010 of $7,718 billion.

- Telecom cost savings in the year 2010, with competition: 16% × $7,718 × 2.0% = $24.70 billion.
- Telecom quality improvement in the year 2010, with competition, $24.70 billion × 1.00 = $24.70 billion.
- Total competition benefits in the year 2010: $49.40 billion.
- Straight-line cumulation of benefits over 14 years = $346 billion.

High-income countries

(excluding those already competitive countries, named in table 1.1): 1993 population 445 million; GNP per capita, 1993 dollars, $23,000; total GNP $10,235 billion; assumed 2.5 percent real annual growth in GNP, 1993-2010 (factor = 1.52) leading to projected GNP in 2010 of $15,557 billion.

- Telecom cost savings in the year 2010, with competition: 16% × $15,557 × 2.0% = $49.78 billion.
- Telecom quality improvement in the year 2010, with competition: $49.78 billion × 0.50 = $24.89 billion.
- Total competition benefits in 2010: $74.67 billion.
- Straight-line cumulation of benefits over 14 years = $523 billion.

Totals

- Worldwide competition benefits, **2010** = $149 billion.
- Straight-line cumulation over 14 years = $1,046 billion.

This procedure is repeated by region to estimate gains by geographic breakdown.

Appendix B:
Final Offers Presented in the NGBT
(30 April 1996)

Final offers presented in the NGBT (30 April 1996)

Country[a]	Market access	Investment	Regulatory principles
Argentina	Open for all services and facilities in 2000.	100% foreign investment permitted.	Some commitments but hasn't adopted reference paper in entirety.
Australia	Open for all services and facilities. Contingent on legislative approval.	Investment limits on Telestra, Vodafone, and Optus.	Adopted in entirety.
Austria	Open	Open	Adopted in entirety.
Barbados	No offer.		
Belgium	Open for all services and facilities except international satellites.	49% investment restriction and limitation on number of suppliers.	Adopted in entirety.
Brazil	Open for closed user groups, paging and domestic international satellite services and facilities, with limitations.	49% limit on investment.	Commitment to bind outcome of future reform legislation.
Canada	Open for all services and facilities except satellites, which will open in 2002.	General 46.7% limit, plus limits on investment in mobile satellite systems.	Adopted in entirety.
Chile	Open market commitments on long-distance, and international service only. No local service commitments.	No limits.	Does not make full commitment on regulatory principles.
Colombia	No offer.		
Cuba	No offer.		
Cyprus	No offer.		
Czech Republic	Open for all services and facilities by 2001.	No limits.	Adopted in entirety.

Country			
Denmark	Open	Open	Adopted in entirety.
Dominican Republic	No commitments.	No commitments.	No commitments.
Ecuador	Open for cellular service only.	No limits.	No commitments.
Egypt	No offer.		
Finland	Open	Open	Adopted in entirety.
France	Open for all services and facilities.	20% investment limit for radio networks and limits on investment in France Telecom.	Adopted in entirety.
Germany	Open	Open	Adopted in entirety.
Greece	Open for all services and facilities by 2003.	No limits.	Adopted in entirety.
Hong Kong	Local wire-line and wireless network services limited to current four providers; international resale of data, closed user groups, call back, and self-provision of external satellite circuits by a company or closed user group permitted. No commitment on open market for local or international public wire-line/wireless services and facilities even after expiration of Hong Kong Telecom's exclusive rights in 2006.	No limits.	Adopted in entirety.

a. **Bold** indicates an offer comparable to that of the United States; 11 countries (including the United States) fall in this category. Six participants (*italicized*) made no offers, and 36 made offers that were short of full liberalization. In all, there were 53 participants. In addition, there were 24 observer nations, listed at the end of the table, that also made no offers.

Final offers presented in the NGBT (30 April 1996) (continued)

Country[a]	Market access	Investment	Regulatory principles
Hungary	Open for all services and facilities by 2002.	75% foreign investment limit.	Adopted in entirety.
Iceland	Open for all services and facilities.	No limits.	No commitments.
India	Duopoly for local and long-distance wire-line, duopoly for cellular. No commitments on international or cellular.	Existing 49% limit to be reduced to 25%.	No commitments.
Ireland	Open for all services and facilities by 2000.	No limits.	Adopted in entirety.
Israel	Open for paging and switched domestic and international resale. Cellular licenses subject to economic needs test. No commitment on local and international wire-line services and satellite service.	Significant limits to investment maintained.	Less than full commitment to regulatory principles.
Italy	Open for all services and facilities.	Limits on investment in STET.	Adopted in entirety.
Ivory Coast	Open for domestic and international data, telegraph, private circuits, mobile and PCS. No commitment on domestic and international voice.	No commitment.	Less than full commitment to regulatory principles.
Japan	Open for all services and facilities.	100% permitted, except for investment in NTT and KDD, which have 20% limit.	Adopted in entirety.

Country			
Korea	Open for all services and facilities except resale, which is to be opened in 2001.	35% limit in all firms except Korea Telecom, which is limited to 20%.	Adopted in entirety.
Luxembourg	Open	Open	Adopted in entirety.
Mauritius	Commitments unclear.		
Mexico	Open market access for local, long-distance and international facilities and services, but no commitment on satellite.	30% investment limit for wire-line and 40% for wireless (down from current limit of 49% for all services).	Does not make full commitment on regulatory principles.
Morocco	Open for domestic packet-switched data, mobile, paging, and PCS. Domestic voice reserved to monopoly until 2002. No commitments on international or satellite services.	No commitments.	No commitments.
Netherlands	Open	Open	Adopted in entirety.
New Zealand	Open	Open	Adopted in entirety.
Norway	Open	Open	Adopted in entirety.
Pakistan	Open for domestic data, telex, and fax. No commitments on local, long-distance, international, or satellite services.	100% investment permitted but no commitment on national treatment.	No commitments.
Peru	Open for all services and facilities by 1999.	No limits.	Adopted in entirety.

Final offers presented in the NGBT (30 April 1996) (continued)

Country[a]	Market access	Investment	Regulatory principles
Philippines	Discretion to limit market access for domestic and international service based on economic needs test. No commitment on satellite services.	40% investment limit.	No commitments.
Poland	Open for domestic data, duopoly for local public voice (wire-line), and cellular. Long-distance services to open by 2003. Open for international data, fax, private leased circuits, and pan-European paging systems. No commitments on international voice (facilities or resale) or satellite services.	100% permitted for local wire-line (voice and data); 49% for cellular, international, and domestic services.	Adopted in entirety.
Portugal	Open for all facilities and services in 2003.	25% investment limit and further limits on investment in privatized state telecom firms.	Adopted in entirety.
Singapore	Open for all facilities and services by 2002, except for international simple resale.	40% foreign investment limits.	Adopted in entirety.
Slovak Republic	Open for all facilities and services by 2003.	40% investment limit for digital cellular.	Adopted in entirety.
Spain	Open for all facilities and services in 2003, though they "may" open by 1998.	25% foreign investment limit for facilities-based or radio-based networks, and investment limit in Telefonica.	Will adopt in entirety by 2003.
Sweden	Open	Open	Adopted in entirety.

Switzerland	Open for domestic and international data, closed user groups, and private leased circuits. Commitment to further open all facilities and services contingent upon legislative authority.	100% investment contingent upon legislative authority.	Adoption contingent upon legislative authority.
Thailand	Open access for local services only, but could bind outcome of reform legislation. No commitments on long-distance, international, or satellite services.	No commitments.	No commitments.
Tunisia	No offer.		
Turkey	No commitment on international satellite services.	No commitments.	No commitments.
United Kingdom	Open	Open	Adopted in entirety.
Venezuela	Open for all facilities and services in 2000.	100% foreign investment permitted.	No commitments.

Observer nations (no offers)
   Bolivia
   Brunei
   Bulgaria
   China
   Chinese Taipei (Taiwan)
   Costa Rica
   El Salvador
   Guatemala
   Honduras

Final offers presented in the NGBT (30 April 1996) (continued)

Country[a]	Market access	Investment	Regulatory principles
Indonesia			
Jamaica			
Latvia			
Madagascar			
Malaysia			
Myanmar (Burma)			
Nicaragua			
Panama			
Romania			
Russian Federation			
Slovenia			
South Africa			
Trinidad and Tobago			
United Arab Emirates			
Uruguay			

Appendix C:
Final Draft of WTO Telecom Regulatory Principles

Negotiating Group on Basic Telecommunications Reference Paper

Scope

The following are definitions and principles on the regulatory framework for the basic telecommunications services.

Definitions

Users mean service consumers and service suppliers.

Essential facilities mean facilities of a public telecommunications transport network or service that

(a) are exclusively or predominantly provided by a single or limited number of suppliers;

(b) cannot feasibly be economically or technically substituted in order to provide a service.

A major supplier is a supplier which has the ability to materially affect the terms of participation (having regard to price and supply) in the market for basic telecommunications service as a result of:

(a) control over essential facilities; or

(b) use of its position in the market.

1. Competitive safeguards

1.1 Prevention of anticompetitive practices in telecommunications

Appropriate measures shall be maintained for the purpose of preventing suppliers who, alone or together, are a major supplier from engaging in or continuing anticompetitive practices.

1.2 Safeguards

The anticompetitive practices referred to above shall include in particular:

(a) engaging in anticompetitive cross-subsidization;

(b) using information obtained from competitors with anticompetitive results; and

(c) not making available to other suppliers on a timely basis technical information about essential facilities and commercially relevant information which are necessary for them to provide services.

2. Interconnection

2.1 This section allies to linking with suppliers providing public telecommunications transport networks or services in order to allow the users of one supplier to communicate with users of another supplier and to access services provided by another supplier, where specific commitments are undertaken.

2.2 Interconnection to be ensured

Interconnection with a major supplier will be ensured at any technically feasible point in the network. Such interconnection is provided:

(a) under nondiscriminatory terms, conditions (including technical standards and specifications), and rates and of a quality no less favorable than that provided for its own like services or for services of nonaffiliated service suppliers or for its subsidiaries or other affiliates;

(b) in a timely fashion, on terms, conditions (including technical standards and specifications), and cost-oriented rates that are transparent, reasonable, having regard to economic feasibility, and sufficiently unbundled so that the supplier need not pay for network components or facilities that it does not require for the service to be provided; and

(c) upon request, at points in addition to the network termination points offered to the majority of users, subject to charges that reflect the cost of construction of necessary additional facilities.

2.3 Public availability of the procedures for interconnection negotiations

The procedures applicable for interconnection to a major supplier will be made publicly available.

2.4 Transparency of interconnection arrangements

It is ensured that a major supplier will make publicly available either its interconnection agreements or a reference interconnection offer.

2.5 Interconnection: dispute settlement

A service supplier requesting interconnection with a major supplier will have recourse, either:

(a) at any time or

(b) after a reasonable period of time which has been made publicly known to an independent domestic body, which may be a regulatory body as referred to in paragraph 5 below, to resolve disputes regarding appropriate terms, conditions and rates for interconnection within a reasonable period of time, to the extent that these have not been established previously.

3. Universal service

Any member has the right to define the kind of universal service obligation it wishes to maintain. Such obligations will not be regarded as anticompetitive per se, provided they are administered in a transparent, nondiscriminatory, and competitively neutral manner and are not more burdensome than necessary for the kind of universal service defined by the member.

4. Public availability of licensing criteria

Where a license is required, the following will be made publicly available:

(a) all the licensing criteria and the period of time normally required to reach a decision concerning an application for a license and

(b) the terms and conditions of individual licenses. The reasons for the denial of a license will be made known to the applicant upon request.

5. Independent regulators

The regulatory body is separate from, and not accountable to, any supplier of basic telecommunications services. The decision of and the procedures used by regulators shall be impartial with respect to all market participants.

6. Allocation and use of scarce resources

Any procedures for the allocation and use of scarce resources, including frequencies, numbers, and rights of way will be carried out in an objective, timely, transparent, and nondiscriminatory manner. The current state of allocated frequency bands will be made publicly available, but detailed identification of frequencies allocated for specific government uses is not required.

Abbreviations and Acronyms

BT	British Telecom
C&W	Cable and Wireless
CANTV	Compañía Anónima Nacional Teléfonos de Venezuela
CNT	Comisión Nacional de Telecomunicaciones
CPE	Customer-premises equipment
CTC	Compañía de Teléfonos de Chile
CTSC	Community Teleservice Centers
DBS	Direct Broadcast Satellite
DoT	Department of Telecommunications (India)
DSU	Dispute Settlement Understanding
ENTel	Empresa Nacional de Telecomunicaciones
FCC	Federal Communications Commission
FLAG	Fiber Link Around the Globe
FWD	Free World Dialup
GNS	Group of Negotiations in Service
HKTC	Hongkong Telecom
IP	Internet Protocol
IRD	Integrated Rural Development
ISDN	Integrated Services Digital Network
ITU	International Telecommunications Union
LEOS	Low Earth Orbit Satellite
MPT	Ministry of Posts and Telecommunications
MSS	Mobile Personal Satellite Services
NGBT	Negotiating Group on Basic Telecommunications
NTT	Nippon Telegraph and Telephone
OSI	Open Systems Interconnection

PBX	Private branch exchange
PLDT	Philippine Long Distance Telephone
PSTN	Public Switched Telephone Network
PTO	Public Telephone Operator
PTT	Post, Telegraph, and Telephone
RBOCs	Regional Bell operating companies
SBC	Southwestern Bell Communications
STET	Societa Finanziaria Telefonica
TELMEX	Teléfonos de México
TCP/IP	Transmission Control Protocol/Internet Protocol
VANS	Value-Added Network Services
VSAT	Very Small Aperture Terminal
WLL	Wireless Local Loop

Glossary

Access charge	Fee imposed by local exchange carriers on interexchange carriers (those unrelated to the host carrier) and on end users to defray that portion of the costs of the local facilities that are associated with, or otherwise assigned to, the provision of interexchange services.
Access line	A telecommunications line that continuously connects a remote station to a switching exchange. A telephone number is associated with the access line.
Accounting rate	The per-minute revenue that is to be "shared" between the originating and terminating parties to an international telecommunications transmission. This is not necessarily based on precise cost factors, but is negotiated between the operators involved. It is generally set in US dollars or other major currency.
Accounting separation	A regulatory requirement by which a telecommunications company must keep separate accounts for each of its network operations and services.

Analog	Signal representations that bear some physical relationship to the original quantity, usually electrical voltage, frequency, resistance, or mechanical translation or rotation.
Backbone network	The main transmission conduit in a particular network system.
Bandwidth	The width of an electrical transmission path or circuit, in terms of the range of frequencies it can accommodate; a measure of the volume of communication traffic that the channel can carry. A voice channel typically has a bandwidth of 4,000 cycles per second (hertz). A TV channel requires about 6.5 megahertz (MHz).
Broadband communication	A specific transmission range, generally having a bandwidth greater than a voice-grade channel and therefore capable of higher speed data transmission.
Broadband integrated services digital network (BISDN)	An optical-fiber-based digital network in which the same switches and transmission paths are used to establish a simultaneous interface for a variety of services, including telephone, data, video, telex, and facsimile.
Broadcast	Simultaneous transmission to a number of stations.
Bypass	Communications that avoid interconnection with part, or all, of the public switched telephone network (PSTN).
Call-back services	An international telecommunications service that bypasses the local telephone provider. After a user calls the call-back service and identifies himself, the computer breaks the connection and calls the user back at a predetermined telephone number with a low-cost foreign dial tone.

Carrier	Any entity that provides telecommunications facilities or services for hire.
Cellular telephone service	A system for handling telephone calls to and from moving users. Cities are divided into small geographic areas known as cells. Telephone calls are transmitted to and from low-power radio transmitters in each cell. Calls are passed from one transmitter to another as the user leaves one cell and enters another.
Central office	The local switch or junction point for a telephone exchange within a public network.
Channel	A means of transmission based on wire, fiber-optic, radio, or other electromagnetic means used to establish a communication link between one point and other. A signal flows in one direction over a given channel, requiring two for back and forth linkage.
Circuit	A combination of two channels that allows bidirectional transmission of signals between two points.
Collection rate	The amount customers are charged for international message toll service (IMTS) calls.
Cross-subsidization	The practice of using surplus revenues generated from one product or service to support another.
Dominant carrier	A regulatory classification for the telecommunications provider that has the largest market share or is otherwise able to exercise market power.
Duopoly	The market situation in which there are only two sellers of a particular good or service.

Economies of scale	The savings in average costs as additional units are added to production. The average cost of providing 100 people with a service, for example, is typically higher than the average cost for providing 1,000 people with the same service.
Economies of scope	When the production of two or more products in a single firm leads to lower costs than when the same volumes of the same products are produced in separate firms.
Electronic data interchange (EDI)	The electronic exchange of trading documents that precludes the need for traditional paper documentation.
Electronic mail (e-mail)	The use of telecommunications for sending textual messages from one person to another. The capacity to store the messages in an electronic mailbox is normally a part of the electronic mail system.
Encryption	Transformation of data from the meaningful code that is normally transmitted (called clear text) to a meaningless sequence of digits and letters that must be decrypted before it becomes meaningful again.
Facilities-based payments	An international accounting settlement mechanism in which the originating operator pays a fee to compensate for the use of a terminating operator's system.
Fiber-optic	Fiber-optic technology is a flexible ultra pure glass fiber the size of human hair that transmits information in the form of pulses of light. Fiber-optic services are differentiated according to the speed of the transmission.
Flat-rate service	A method of charging for local calls that gives the user an unlimited number of calls for a fixed monthly fee.

Gateway	The connection between two networks that use different protocols. The gateway translates the protocols to allow terminals on the two networks to communicate.
Global System for Mobile Communications (GSM)	Originally called Groupe Speciale Mobile, this is a European digital cellular standard.
High-speed circuit	A circuit designed to carry data at speeds greater than voice-grade circuits.
Hub	A point at which communications transmissions switch or transit.
Integrated services digital network (ISDN)	A network in which the same switches and transmission paths are used to establish a simultaneous interface for a variety of services, including telephone, data, video, telex, and facsimile.
International direct dialing (IDD)	A computer-based dialing system used for international telecommunications services.
International Telecommunications Union (ITU)	A multinational organization and agency of the United Nations, established to standardize communications procedures and practices among national telecommunications administrations, including frequency allocation and radio regulations.
Internet	A global "network of interconnected networks," whose components belong to various government, research, education, and private organizations that transmits data, image, and voice in an open systems environment.
Leased circuits	A dedicated circuit made available at bulk rate to users requiring exclusive or continuous capacity for high-speed transmission.
Local-area network (LAN)	A telecommunications network (public or private) that grants services in an authorized local area and connects with the public network to provide long-distance services.

Local loop	A line connecting a customer's telephone equipment with the local telephone exchange.
Long-distance service	A telecommunications transmission service, particularly telephone service, that connects locations that cannot be reached with a local telephone call—that is, which lie outside each other's local exchange area.
Low Earth Orbit Satellites (LEOS)	Communications satellites, usually in an array of multiple units, providing ubiquitous point-to-point telecommunications service.
Market access	A commitment by a WTO member country to open its market to service suppliers from other member countries.
Mobile services	Radio communication services between ships, aircraft, vehicles, or other stations for use while they are moving or between such stations and fixed points on land.
Monopoly	A market with only one firm selling a given good or service. No other firms sell closely related goods or services in the same markets.
Most-favored nation (MFN)	A WTO principle that, in the case of telecommunications, requires that service suppliers from any one WTO member be given no less market access than is extended to suppliers from any other member.
National treatment	A WTO principle under which member countries may subject foreign companies to conditions no more onerous than those imposed on domestic firms.
Number portability	A network feature permitting a customer to retain a telephone number when changing residence or location (geographical portability) or telecom service provider (operator portability).
Online	The state of being actively connected to a network or computer system and able to interactively exchange commands, data, and information with a host device.

Open network architecture (ONA)	A standard that allows telecommunications vendors to connect with a network.
Open Systems Interconnection	A network accessible to all service providers wishing to attach to it.
Packet-switched data network	An efficient data transmission system whereby messages are broken down into smaller units, or bundles, that are transmitted separately along the most direct route available and then reassembled at their destination.
Paging system	A radio communication technology used to send messages point-to-point in only one direction, generally with the purpose of sending a short message to a mobile receiver.
Personal communications service (PCS)	A type of communication in which a user carries a small communications unit that can be reached regardless of location. The system has advanced digital features that allows for high customization of services.
Post, Telephone, and Telegraph (PTT)	See PTO.
Price-cap regulation	A method of regulating prices whereby a "cap" is placed on the prices of a basket of services, with annual increases tied to an inflation factor.
Private branch exchange (PBX)	A "dedicated" telephone exchange in an organization requiring multiple lines; it offers features such as automatic call distribution and call waiting.
Private network	A telecommunications network established by businesses (individuals or institutions) with their own hardware or through the lease of public network channels and circuits for intra- or interfirm communication.
Privatization	The transfer of commercially oriented state-owned government enterprises, activities, or productive assets to partial or total private ownership or control.

Public call office (PCO)	A telephone facility available for public use, generally on payment of a fee to an attendant or a coin box.
Public switched telephone network (PSTN)	A telecommunications network used to provide service to the public in general. It does not include customer premises equipment, local-area networks, or private branch exchanges.
Public telephone operator (PTO)	A generic term for government-operated common carriers.
Radio spectrum	The portion of the electromagnetic spectrum within which frequencies can be generated and detected by electronic means.
Rate-of-return regulation	The regulation of prices that carriers charge, based on fixing the rate of return, on the carrier's investment or rate base.
Regulation	The process of ensuring that public utilities—such as common carriers—operate in accordance with an established framework of rules. These rules may govern the offering of service by a carrier and include practices, classifications, and definitions.
Regulatory agency	An agency empowered to control and monitor the commercial activities of radio and television broadcasters, cable system operators, telecommunications carriers, or any other public utility in the public interest.
Resale	The sale or lease on a commercial basis, with or without adding value, of telecommunications services leased from a telecommunications carrier.
Settlement rate	The proportion of the accounting rate—usually 50 percent—paid by the sending telephone administration to the receiving telephone administration.
Structural separation	The requirement that a company providing services in various segments of the market (i.e., basic voice services,

	value-added services, mobile cellular services, etc.) create separate subsidiaries with independent administration, accounting, and record keeping operations.
Switch	The process or equipment that connects telecommunications channels or circuits to allow the transmission of signals.
Symmetry	A condition wherein a dominant carrier can claim the same interconnection rights as those it must grant to new entrants.
Tariff	The published rate for a specific unit of equipment, facility, or type of service provided by a telecommunications carrier.
Telecommunications network	The infrastructure that provides channels and circuits to conduct voice, data, or video signals between two points.
Teledensity	The number of access lines relative to population.
Universal service	The concept that every individual within a country should have basic telephone service available at an affordable price.
Value-added network service (VANS)	The telecommunications services provided through private or public networks—generally based on packet-switching technology—with a computer-based information feature or performance that provides services such as electronic mail or voice mail.
Very small aperture terminal (VSAT)	A satellite-based technology used primarily for data transmission.
Videoconferencing	Using multiparty audio-video communications over a telecommunications network.
Volume-based payments	Compensation paid in an international telecommunications transmission by the sending country that is tied to the volume of calls sent on a descending scale to encourage low collection charges on outgoing traffic.

Wireless local loop (WLL)   A wireless, radio-based technology that connects subscribers to a public telephone exchange and allows them to make local calls.

References

Aamoth, Robert J. 1995. "International Accounting Rates: Where Do We Go From Here and How Do We Get There?" Paper presented at the Economist Roundtable on Telecommunications, 14 June, Hong Kong.

Aronson, Jonathan, and Peter Cowhey. 1988. *When Countries Talk: Trade in Communications Services.* Cambridge: Ballinger.

Bice, Steven D., Greg Dever, Lori Mukaida, Scott Norton, and Jimione Samisone. 1996. "Telemedicine and Telehealth in the Pacific Islands Region: A Survey of Applications, Experiments, and Issues." Proceedings of the 18th Annual Pacific Telecommunications Conference, 14–18 January, Hawaii.

Cameron, Kelly, and Peter Cowhey. 1996. "What Would an NGBT Deal Require?" Paper presented at the Institute for International Economics Conference on Liberalizing Telecommunications Services, 29 January, Washington.

Clark, Theodore H., and James L. McKenney. 1995. *Linking the Grocery Channel: Management Issues of Implementing Interorganizational Connectivity.* Harvard Business School Working Paper No. 95-019. Cambridge, MA: Harvard University.

Crandall, Robert W. 1996. "Telecom Mergers and Joint Ventures in an Era of Liberalization." Paper presented at the Institute for International Economics Conference on Liberalizing Telecommunications Services, 29 January, Washington.

Cronin, Francis J., Edwin B. Parker, Elisabeth K. Coleran, and Mark A. Gold. 1991. "Telecommunications Infrastructure and Economic Growth: An Analysis of Causality." *Telecommunications Policy* 15, no. 6: 529–35.

Cronin, Francis J., Edwin B. Parker, Elisabeth K. Coleran, and Mark A. Gold. 1993. "Telecommunications Infrastructure Investment and Economic Development." *Telecommunications Policy* 17, no. 6: 415–30.

Dhalokia, Ruby R., and Bari Harlam. 1994. "Telecommunications and Economic Development: Econometric Analysis of the US Experience." *Telecommunications Policy* 18, no. 6: 470–77.

Dordick, Herbert S., and Marilyn Diane Fife. 1991. "Universal Service in Post-Divestiture USA." *Telecommunications Policy* 15, no. 2: 119–28.

Drake, William, and Karen Frazer. 1996. "The Internet and the Transformation of Global Telecommunications." Paper presented at the Institute for International Economics Conference on Liberalizing Telecommunications Services, 29 January, Washington.

Drake, William J., and Kalypso Nicolaïdis. 1992. "Ideas, Interest, and Institutionalization: 'Trade in Service' and the Uruguay Round." *International Organization* 46, no. 1 (Winter): 37–86.

Ergas, Henry. 1996. "International Trade in Telecommunications Services: An Economic Perspective." Paper presented at the Institute for International Economics Conference on Liberalizing Telecommunications Services, 29 January, Washington.

Ergas, Henry, and Paul Paterson. 1991. "International Telecommunications Settlement Arrangements: An Unsustainable Inheritance?" *Telecommunications Policy* 15, no. 1 (February): 29–48.

Federal Communications Commission (FCC). 1996. "Policy Statement on International Accounting Rate Reform." Washington (31 January).

Forge, Simon. 1995. *Consequences of Current Telecommunications Trends on the Competitiveness of Developing Countries*. Washington: World Bank.

Frieden, Robert. 1993. "International Toll Revenue Division: Tackling the Inequities and Inefficiencies." *Telecommunications Policy* 17, no. 3 (April): 221–33.

Frieden, Robert. 1996. "The Impact of Boomerang Boxes and Callback Services on the Accounting Rate Regime." Proceedings of the 18th Annual Pacific Telecommunications Conference, 14–18 January, Hawaii.

Globerman, Steven. 1995. "Foreign Ownership in Telecommunications: A Policy Perspective." *Telecommunications Policy* 19, no. 1: 21–28.

Goussal, Dario. 1996. "A Second Look at CTCS." Proceedings of the 18th Annual Pacific Telecommunications Conference, 14–18 January, Hawaii.

Graham, Edward M., and Robert Z. Lawrence. 1996. "Measuring the Contestability of Markets: A Conceptual Approach." Paper for the OECD Committee on International Trade, 14 February, Paris.

Hanna, Nagy. 1993. *Exploiting Information Technology for Development: A Case Study of India.* World Bank Discussion Paper No. 246. Washington: World Bank.

Hardy, Andrew. 1980. "The Role of the Telephone in Economic Development." *Telecommunications Policy* 4, no. 4: 278–86.

Harindranath, G., and Jonathan Liebenau. 1995. "State Policy and India's Software Industry in the 1990s." In M. Khosrowpour, *Managing Information and Communications in a Changing Global Environment*. London: Idea Group Publishing.

Harper, J. M. 1995. "The Case Against Competing Infrastructure." *Telecommunications Policy* 19, no. 4: 285–98.

Horwitz, Robert B. 1989. *The Irony of Regulatory Reform: The Deregulation of American Telecommunications*. New York: Oxford University Press.

Hudson, Heather. 1988. "Generating Foreign Exchange in Developing Countries: The Potential of Telecommunications Investments." *Telecommunications Policy* 12, no. 3: 272–78.

Hudson, Heather. 1994. "Applications of Telecommunications for the Delivery of Social Services." In Robert Saunders, Jeremy Warford, and Bjorn Wellenius, *Telecommunications and Economic Development*. Baltimore: Johns Hopkins University Press.

Hudson, Heather. 1995. "Economic and Social Benefits of Rural Telecommunications—A Report to the World Bank." Unpublished report. Washington: World Bank.

Ibarra, Alejandro. 1996. "Telecommunications Trends in Mexico and Latin America." Paper presented at the Institute for International Economics Conference on Liberalizing Telecommunications Services, 29 January, Washington.

International Telecommunications Union (ITU). 1988. *Contribution of Telecommunications to the Savings of Foreign Exchange in Developing Countries*. Geneva.

International Telecommunications Union (ITU). 1993. Options for Regulatory Processes and Procedures in Telecommunications. Geneva.

International Telecommunications Union (ITU). 1995a. *Telecommunications Indicators for Least Developed Countries*. Geneva.

International Telecommunications Union (ITU). 1995b. *World Telecommunications Development Report: Information Infrastructures.* Geneva.

International Telecommunications Union (ITU). 1995c. *World Telecommunications Indicators.* Geneva.

International Telecommunications Union (ITU). 1996. *Trade Agreements on Telecommunications: Regulatory Implications.* Geneva.

Kelly, Tim. 1996. "Forecasting the Mobile Communications Market: A Finger in the Airwaves?" Paper presented at the International Institute for Research Conference on Market Forecasting in the Telecoms Industry, 11–13 March, Hong Kong.

Lichtensztejn, Samuel. 1990. "Inversion Extranjera Directa por Deuda Externa: ¿Freno Impulso de la Crisis en América Latina?" (Foreign Direct Investment for External Debt: Halt or Trigger of the Latin American Crisis?). In Carlos Tello Macias and Clemente Ruiz Durán, *Crisis Financiera y Mecanismos de Contención (Financial Crisis and Contentment Mechanisms).* Mexico, D.F.: Fondo de Cultura Económica.

Lovelock, Peter. 1995. "Understanding China's Telecommunications: The Case of the 1997 Hong Kong Transition." Paper presented at the Hong Kong University of Science and Technoloy Conference on Future Telecommunications, 20 November, Hong Kong.

Luders, Rolf. 1996. "Did Privatization Raise Enterprise Efficiency in Chile?" In William Glade, *Economic and Social Impact of Privatization in Latin America.* Boulder: Westview Press. Forthcoming.

McCormack, Arthur. 1980. *Multinational Investment: Boon and Burden for Developing Countries?* New York: W. R. Grace & Co.

Malgavkar, P. D., and V. K. Chebbi. 1988. "Impact of Telecommunications Facility on Rural Development in India." Proceedings of the 10th Pacific Telecommunications Conference, 14–18 January, Hawaii.

Melo, José Ricardo. 1994. "Liberalization and Privatization in Chile." In Bjorn Wellenius and Peter A. Stern, *Implementing Reforms in the Telecommunications Sector: Lessons from Experience.* Washington: World Bank.

Melody, William H. 1993. "The Overlooked Opportunity: Rural and Remote Area Telecoms." *Pacific Telecommunications Review* (December).

Mody, Bella, Johannes Bauer, and Joseph Straubhaar. 1995. *Telecommunications Politics: Ownership and Control of the Information Highway in Developing Countries.* Nahwah, NJ: LEA Publishers.

Moran, Theodore H. 1986. *Investing in Development: New Roles for Private Capital?* Washington: Overseas Development Council.

Mueller, Milton. 1993. "Universal Service in Telephone History: A Reconstruction." *Telecommunications Policy* 17, no. 5: 352–69.

Mueller, Milton. 1996. *Universal Service: Interconnection, Competition, and Monopoly in the Making of the American Telephone System.* Washington: MIT Press. Forthcoming.

Nair, Govindan. 1995. *Mauritius: Towards an Information Based Economy.* Washington: World Bank.

Null, Roger, and Frances Rosenbluth. 1995. "Telecommunications Policy: Structure, Process, Outcomes." In Petu Cowhey and Matthew McCubbins, *Structure and Policy in Japan and the United States.* Cambridge, MA: Cambridge University Press.

Office of Telecommunications (OFTEL). 1994. *Interconnection and Accounting Separation: The Next Steps.* London: OFTEL.

Organization for Economic Cooperation and Development (OECD). 1995a. *Restructuring in Public Telecommunications Operator Employment.* Paris: OECD.

Organization for Economic Cooperation and Development (OECD). 1995b. *Telecommunications Infrastructure: The Benefits of Competition.* Paris: OECD.

Organization for Economic Cooperation and Development (OECD). 1995c. *The Impact of Telecommunications Globalization on Domestic Policy.* Paris: OECD.

Organization for Economic Cooperation and Development (OECD). 1996. *Information Infrastructure Convergence and Pricing: The Internet*. Paris.

Ovum Ltd. 1994. *Number Portability: Numbering for Consumer Benefit in Hong Kong*. Report to the Office of the Telecommunications Authority. Hong Kong: OFTA.

Pepper, Robert. 1995. "Competition and Reinventing Regulation." Paper presented at the Programme on Information and Communication Technologies International Conference on the Social and Economic Implications of Information and Communications Technologies, May, Westminster, London.

Petrazzini, Ben A. 1995. *The Political Economy of Telecommunications Reform in Developing Countries: Privatization and Liberalization in Comparative Perspective*. Westport, CT: Praeger.

Petrazzini, Ben A., and Theodore K. Clark. 1996a. "Costs and Benefits of Telecommunications Liberalization in Developing Countries." Paper presented at the Institute for International Economics Conference on Liberalizing Telecommunications, 29 January, Washington.

Petrazzini, Ben A., and Theodore K. Clark. 1996b. "Evolving Telecommunications Regulatory Regimes in Developing Countries." Proceedings of the 18th Pacific Telecommunications Conference, 14–18 January, Hawaii.

Petrazzini, Ben A., and G. Harindranath. 1996. "Information Infrastructure Initiatives in Emerging Economies: The Case of India." In Brian Kahin, *National and International Initiatives for Information Infrastructure*. Cambridge: MIT Press. Forthcoming.

Pipe, Russell G. 1993. *Trade of Telecommunications Services: Implications of a GATT Uruguay Round Agreement for ITU and Member States*. Report prepared for the International Telecommunications Union. Geneva: ITU.

Preston, Paschal. 1995. "Competition in the Telecommunications Infrastructure." *Telecommunications Policy* 19, no. 4: 253–71.

Qvortrup, Lars. 1989. "The Nordic Telecottages: Community Teleservice Centres for Rural Regions." *Telecommunications Policy* 13, no. 1: 59–68.

Ramamurti, Ravi, ed. 1995. *The Privatization of Infrastructure in Developing Countries: Lessons from Latin America*. Baltimore: Johns Hopkins University Press.

Richter, Walter. 1995. "Economic Justification for Telecommunications Investment in Developing Countries." Manuscript. Geneva: International Telecommunications Union.

Saunders, Robert, Jeremy Warford, and Bjorn Wellenius. 1994. *Telecommunications and Economic Development*. Baltimore: Johns Hopkins University Press.

Savage, James. 1996. "The Future of the International Telecommunications Accounting Rate Regime." Proceedings of the 18th Annual Pacific Telecommunications Conference, 14–18 January, Hawaii.

Schott, Jeffrey J. 1994. *Uruguay Round: An Assessment*. Washington: Institute for International Economics.

Solomon, Jonathan, and Dawson Walker. 1995. "Separating Infrastructure and Service Provision: The Broadband Imperative." *Telecommunications Policy* 19, no. 2: 83–89.

Stehmann, Oliver. 1995. "Network Liberalization and Developing Countries: The Case of Chile." *Telecommunications Policy* 19, no. 9: 667–84.

Stone, Alan. 1989. *Wrong Number: The Break Up of AT&T*. New York: Basic Books.

Talero, E., and P. Gauddette. 1995. "Harnessing Information for Development." Unpublished manuscript. Washington: World Bank.

Tandon, Pankaj, and Manuel Abdala. 1992. "Mexico: Teléfonos de México." In Ahmed Galal, Leroy Jones, Pankaj Tandon, and Ingo Vogelsang, *Welfare Consequences of Selling Public Enterprises: Case Studies from Chile, Malaysia, Mexico, and the U.K.* Washington: World Bank.

Todaro, Michael. 1981. *Economic Development in the Third World*. New York: Longman.

United Nations Development Program (UNDP). 1995. *Human Development Report*. New York: Oxford University Press.

Ure, John, ed. 1995. *Telecommunications in Asia: Policy, Planning, and Development.* Hong Kong: Hong Kong University Press.

Venturelli, Shalini. 1996. "The Political-Competitive Order of Information Liberalization in the European Union." Proceedings of the National and International Initiatives for Information Infrastructure, Harvard University, 25–27 January, Cambridge, MA.

Wellenius, Bjorn, et al. 1993. *Telecommunications: World Bank Experience and Strategy.* World Bank Discussion Paper No. 192. Washington: World Bank.

Wellenius, Bjorn, and Peter A. Stern. 1994. *Implementing Reforms in the Telecommunications Sector: Lessons from Experience.* Washington: World Bank.

Wolhers de Almeida, Marcio. 1994. "Reestructuracao, Internacionalizacao e Mudancas Institucionais das Telecomunicacoes: Licoes das Experiencias Internacionais para o Caso Brasileiro" (Restructuring, Internationalization, and Institutional Changes in Telecommunications: Lessons from International Experiences for the Brazilian Case). Ph.D. dissertation, Universidade Estadual de Campinas, Sao Paulo, Brazil.

Other Publications from the
Institute for International Economics

BOOKS

IMF Conditionality
John Williamson, editor/*1983*   ISBN cloth 0-88132-006-4   695 pp.

Trade Policy in the 1980s
William R. Cline, editor/*1983*
(out of print)   ISBN paper 0-88132-031-5   810 pp.

Subsidies in International Trade
Gary Clyde Hufbauer and Joanna Shelton Erb/*1984*
                              ISBN cloth 0-88132-004-8   299 pp.

International Debt: Systemic Risk and Policy Response
William R. Cline/*1984*   ISBN cloth 0-88132-015-3   336 pp.

Trade Protection in the United States: 31 Case Studies
Gary Clyde Hufbauer, Diane E. Berliner, and Kimberly Ann Elliott/*1986*
(out of print)   ISBN paper 0-88132-040-4   371 pp.

Toward Renewed Economic Growth in Latin America
Bela Balassa, Gerardo M. Bueno, Pedro-Pablo Kuczynski,
and Mario Henrique Simonsen/*1986*
(out of stock)   ISBN paper 0-88132-045-5   205 pp.

Capital Flight and Third World Debt
Donald R. Lessard and John Williamson, editors/*1987*
(out of print)   ISBN paper 0-88132-053-6   270 pp.

The Canada-United States Free Trade Agreement:
The Global Impact
Jeffrey J. Schott and Murray G. Smith, editors/*1988*
                              ISBN paper 0-88132-073-0   211 pp.

World Agricultural Trade: Building a Consensus
William M. Miner and Dale E. Hathaway, editors/*1988*
                              ISBN paper 0-88132-071-3   226 pp.

Japan in the World Economy
Bela Balassa and Marcus Noland/*1988*
                              ISBN paper 0-88132-041-2   306 pp.

America in the World Economy: A Strategy for the 1990s
C. Fred Bergsten/*1988*   ISBN cloth 0-88132-089-7   235 pp.
                              ISBN paper 0-88132-082-X   235 pp.

Managing the Dollar: From the Plaza to the Louvre
Yoichi Funabashi/*1988, 2d ed. 1989*
                              ISBN paper 0-88132-097-8   307 pp.

United States External Adjustment and the World Economy
William R. Cline/*May 1989* ISBN paper 0-88132-048-X   392 pp.

Free Trade Areas and U.S. Trade Policy
Jeffrey J. Schott, editor/*May 1989*   ISBN paper 0-88132-094-3   400 pp.

Dollar Politics: Exchange Rate Policymaking in the United States
I. M. Destler and C. Randall Henning/*September 1989*
(out of print)   ISBN paper 0-88132-079-X   192 pp.

Latin American Adjustment: How Much Has Happened?
John Williamson, editor/*April 1990*
                              ISBN paper 0-88132-125-7   480 pp.

The Future of World Trade in Textiles and Apparel
William R. Cline/*1987, 2d ed. June 1990*
                              ISBN paper 0-88132-110-9   344 pp.

**Completing the Uruguay Round: A Results-Oriented Approach
to the GATT Trade Negotiations**
Jeffrey J. Schott, editor/*September 1990*
                              ISBN paper 0-88132-130-3   256 pp.

Economic Sanctions Reconsidered (in two volumes)
  Economic Sanctions Reconsidered: Supplemental Case Histories
  Gary Clyde Hufbauer, Jeffrey J. Schott, and Kimberly Ann Elliott/*1985, 2d ed.*
    December 1990   ISBN cloth 0-88132-115-X   928 pp.
                              ISBN paper 0-88132-105-2   928 pp.

  Economic Sanctions Reconsidered: History and Current Policy
  Gary Clyde Hufbauer, Jeffrey J. Schott, and Kimberly Ann Elliott/*December 1990*
                              ISBN cloth 0-88132-136-2   288 pp.
                              ISBN paper 0-88132-140-0   288 pp.

Pacific Basin Developing Countries: Prospects for the Future
Marcus Noland/*January 1991*   ISBN cloth 0-88132-141-9   250 pp.
(out of print)   ISBN paper 0-88132-081-1   250 pp.

Currency Convertibility in Eastern Europe
John Williamson, editor/*October 1991*
                              ISBN paper 0-88132-128-1   396 pp.

International Adjustment and Financing: The Lessons of 1985-1991
C. Fred Bergsten, editor/*January 1992*
                              ISBN paper 0-88132-112-5   336 pp.

North American Free Trade: Issues and Recommendations
Gary Clyde Hufbauer and Jeffrey J. Schott/*April 1992*
                              ISBN paper 0-88132-120-6   392 pp.

Narrowing the U.S. Current Account Deficit
Allen J. Lenz/*June 1992*
(out of print)   ISBN paper 0-88132-103-6   640 pp.

The Economics of Global Warming
William R. Cline/*June 1992* ISBN paper 0-88132-132-X   416 pp.

U.S. Taxation of International Income: Blueprint for Reform
Gary Clyde Hufbauer, assisted by Joanna M. van Rooij/*October 1992*
                              ISBN cloth 0-88132-178-8   304 pp.
                              ISBN paper 0-88132-134-6   304 pp.

Who's Bashing Whom? Trade Conflict in High-Technology Industries
Laura D'Andrea Tyson/*November 1992*
                              ISBN paper 0-88132-106-0   352 pp.
Korea in the World Economy
Il SaKong/*January 1993*
                              ISBN paper 0-88132-106-0   328 pp.
Pacific Dynamism and the International Economic System
C. Fred Bergsten and Marcus Noland, editors/*May 1993*
                              ISBN paper 0-88132-196-6   424 pp.

Economic Consequences of Soviet Disintegration
John Williamson, editor/*May 1993*
                              ISBN paper 0-88132-190-7   664 pp.

Measuring the Costs of Protection in Japan
Yoko Sazanami, Shujiro Urata, and Hiroki Kawai/*January 1995*
ISBN paper 0-88132-211-3   96 pp.

Foreign Direct Investment in the United States, Third Edition
Edward M. Graham and Paul R. Krugman/*January 1995*
ISBN paper 0-88132-204-0   232 pp.

The Political Economy of Korea-United States Cooperation
C. Fred Bergsten and Il SaKong, editors/*February 1995*
ISBN paper 0-88132-213-X   128 pp.

International Debt Reexamined
William R. Cline/*February 1995*
ISBN paper 0-88132-083-8   560 pp.

American Trade Politics, Third Edition
I. M. Destler/*April 1995*   ISBN paper 0-88132-215-6   360 pp.

Managing Official Export Credits: The Quest for a Global Regime
John E. Ray/*July 1995*   ISBN paper 0-88132-207-5   344 pp.

Asia Pacific Fusion: Japan's Role in APEC
Yoichi Funabashi/*October 1995*
ISBN paper 0-88132-224-5   312 pp.

Korea-United States Cooperation in the New World Order
C. Fred Bergsten and Il SaKong, editors/*February 1996*
ISBN paper 0-88132-226-1   144 pp.

Why Exports Really Matter!   ISBN paper 0-88132-221-0   34 pp.
Why Exports Matter More!   ISBN paper 0-88132-229-6   36 pp.
J. David Richardson and Karin Rindal/*July 1995; February 1996*

Global Corporations and National Governments
Edward M. Graham/*May 1996*   ISBN paper 0-88132-111-7   168 pp.

Global Economic Leadership and the Group of Seven
C. Fred Bergsten and C. Randall Henning/*May 1996*
ISBN paper 0-88132-218-0   192 pp.

SPECIAL REPORTS
1   Promoting World Recovery: A Statement on Global Economic Strategy
    by Twenty-six Economists from Fourteen Countries/*December 1982*
    (out of print)   ISBN paper 0-88132-013-7   45 pp.
2   Prospects for Adjustment in Argentina, Brazil, and Mexico:
    Responding to the Debt Crisis   (out of print)
    John Williamson, editor/*June 1983*   ISBN paper 0-88132-016-1   71 pp.
3   Inflation and Indexation: Argentina, Brazil, and Israel
    John Williamson, editor/*March 1985*   ISBN paper 0-88132-037-4   191 pp.
4   Global Economic Imbalances
    C. Fred Bergsten, editor/*March 1986*   ISBN cloth 0-88132-038-2   126 pp.
    ISBN paper 0-88132-042-0   126 pp.
5   African Debt and Financing
    Carol Lancaster and John Williamson, editors/*May 1986*
    (out of print)   ISBN paper 0-88132-044-7   229 pp.
6   Resolving the Global Economic Crisis: After Wall Street
    Thirty-three Economists from Thirteen Countries/*December 1987*
    ISBN paper 0-88132-070-6   30 pp.
7   World Economic Problems
    Kimberly Ann Elliott and John Williamson, editors/*April 1988*
    ISBN paper 0-88132-055-2   298 pp.

Reforming World Agricultural Trade
Twenty-nine Professionals from Seventeen Countries/1988
ISBN paper 0-88132-088-9   42 pp.

8   Economic Relations Between the United States and Korea:
    Conflict or Cooperation?
    Thomas O. Bayard and Soo-Gil Young, editors/*January 1989*
                ISBN paper 0-88132-068-4   192 pp.

WORKS IN PROGRESS

Private Capital Flows to Emerging Markets after the Mexican Crisis
Guillermo Calvo, Morris Goldstein, and Eduard Hochreiter

Trade, Jobs, and Income Distribution
William R. Cline

Trade and Labor Standards
Kimberly Ann Elliott and Richard Freeman

Regional Trading Blocs in the World Economic System
Jeffrey A. Frankel

Transatlantic Free Trade Agreement
Ellen Frost

Forecasting Financial Crises: Early Warning Signs for Emerging Markets
Morris Goldstein and Carmen Reinhart

Overseeing Global Capital Markets
Morris Goldstein and Peter Garber

Global Competition Policy
Edward M. Graham and J. David Richardson

Flying High: Civil Aviation in the Asia Pacific
Gary Clyde Hufbauer and Christopher Findlay

Toward an Asia Pacific Economic Community?
Gary Clyde Hufbauer and Jeffrey J. Schott

The Economics of Korean Unification
Marcus Noland

The Case for Trade: A Modern Reconsideration
J. David Richardson

The Future of the World Trading System
John Whalley and Colleen Hamilton

Crawling Bands: Lessons from Chile, Colombia, and Israel
John Williamson

For orders outside the US and Canada please contact:

    Longman Group UK Ltd.   Telephone Orders: 0279 623923
    PO Box 88, Fourth Avenue   Fax: 0279 453450   Telex: 81259
    Harlow, Essex CM 19 5SR   UK

Canadian customers can order from the Institute or from either:

RENOUF BOOKSTORE	LA LIBERTÉ
1294 Algoma Road	3020 chemin Sainte-Foy
Ottawa, Ontario K1B 3W8	Quebec G1X 3V6
Telephone: (613) 741-4333	Telephone: (418) 658-3763
Fax: (613) 741-5439	Fax: (800) 567-5449

Visit our website at: http://www.iie.com   E-mail address: orders@iie.com